Twin Souls

Twin Souls

Finding Your True Spiritual Partner

Patricia Joudry and Maurie D. Pressman, M.D.

BOOKPLACE

HAZELDEN®

INFORMATION & EDUCATIONAL SERVICES

Hazelden
Center City, Minnesota 55012-0176

1-800-328-0094
1-651-213-4590 (Fax)
www.hazelden.org

(Originally titled *Twin Souls: A Guide to Finding Your True
    Spiritual Partner*)
Published by Somerville House Canada, 1993
Published by Carol Southern Books, an imprint of
    Crown Publishers, Inc., 1995
Published by Hazelden, 2000
Printed in the United States of America

Library of Congress Cataloging-in-Publication Data

Joudry, Patricia, 1921–
    Twin souls : finding your true spiritual partner / Patricia Joudry and
    Maurie D. Pressman.

        p. cm.
    Includes index.
    ISBN 1-56838-569-2 (paperback)
    I. Soul mates. I. Pressman, Maurie D. II. Title.

BF1045.I58 J68 2000
291.2'2—dc21

                                                    00-044978

Editor's note
All the stories in this book are based on actual experiences. In certain cases,
the names and details have been changed to protect the privacy of the people
involved.

04 03 02 01 00   6 5 4 3 2

Cover design by David Spohn
Interior design by Wendy Holdman
Typesetting by Stanton Publication Services, Inc.

We lovingly dedicate this book to Lucinda Vardey

Contents

Introduction

ON A NIGHT IN JULY 1960, AS I SAT MEDITAT-
ing, the twin-soul picture came to me in a vision. I saw
it whole, in an instant: the splitting of the soul into its
twin halves, masculine and feminine, the long evolution back together, and the all-encompassing cosmic
plan of group-soul division and return. All of the details were there, indelibly impressed upon my mind.
Some of it would later sink below the surface, to rise at
various times when called upon.

I had never heard of the twin-soul idea before. Yet
it came with the conviction that I was being given a
task: put it into writing. I saw that my years as a writer
and spiritual seeker had served as preparation for this
work.

Eager to find what had already been written, I
began my search through the spiritual literature. I
could find nothing except an occasional brief refer-
ence, indicating that twinsoulship was known in certain esoteric circles. Like pieces of a puzzle, each fitted

neatly into the pattern I had been shown. None went beyond it. And nowhere did I find the whole of the plan set forth.

I spoke to people about twin souls, relaying the substance of my vision. In some, there was an immediate response. They would begin to smile and nod their heads, murmuring, "Yes . . . yes . . . I'm sure it's true," indicating a knowledge already present in the mind, but now rediscovered.

For thirty years I lived intimately with the twin-soul principle, meditating on it, studying it inwardly, seeking other sources. I made several attempts to write a book but could not seem to capture the subject satisfactorily on paper. There was something missing. The twin-soul theme crept subtly into my other books; it had become a part of me from my deep conviction of its truth.

In October 1989 I met Dr. Maurie Pressman, psychoanalyst and man of the spirit. He, too, was interested in literature. We found that our spiritual paths had been running parallel. We were both particularly interested in the study of Theosophy, the wisdom of the ancient masters. We became friends. I described for him my vision of long ago. His understanding of the male and female psyche brought the missing dimension to the twin-soul concept. He was able to ground the theory, bringing it into the realm of life as it is lived. As we pursued the subject together, the book that had eluded me all those years finally took shape.

What we have written here is hardly the last word on twinsoulship; it is only a beginning. There is much more to be discovered about this beneficent law of love. As you read, you will have insights of your own. Trust them. They will be the voices of your intuition.

In Bernard Shaw's *Saint Joan,* the Inquisitor challenges Joan with: "Your voices are only in your imagination." She replies: "Of course. How else does God speak to us?"

— Patricia Joudry

"The supreme state of human love is . . .
the unity of one soul in two bodies."
— *Sri Aurobindo*

The Soul's Purpose

"Whatever our souls are made of, his and mine are the same.
He is more myself than I am! . . . I am Heathcliff."

THIS PURE TWIN-SOUL UTTERANCE WAS MADE by Cathy in *Wuthering Heights,* a classic love story written by a lonely spinster with no apparent experience of love. Emily Brontë's inspiration came from her soul. This same soul knowledge has inspired all the great love stories of literature and opera. Such works endure because their central truth touches the deeply buried truth in all of us: we are incomplete and there exists somewhere a completing other who will make us whole, as we were whole in the beginning.

The spiritual philosophies of the East, contained in the Bhagavad Gita, the Hindu Vedas, and other writings of the ancient masters, teach us that the soul was created containing both masculine and feminine in one, reflecting the dual nature of the Creator.

The idea of the soul's division into two genders has

come down to us through the ages in the words of philosophers, poets, and spiritual teachers. As a principle of nature, the nineteenth-century philosopher Arthur Schopenhauer described it this way: "Polarity or the sundering of a force into its equal and opposite halves, is a fundamental type of all the phenomena of Nature, from the crystal and the magnet to man himself."

The twin-soul image was graphically portrayed by Plato twenty-five centuries ago, in a legend that has caught and held the imagination of the Western world. In the *Symposium,* Aristophanes speaks in praise of love, relating how Zeus struck the soul into two opposite halves, each to wander the earth in search of the other.

> And when one of them meets with his other half, the actual half of himself, the pair are lost in an amazement of love and friendship and intimacy and one will not be out of the other's sight even for a moment. These are the people who pass their whole lives together; yet they could not explain what they desire of one another. For the intense yearning which each of them has towards the other does not appear to be the desire of lover's intercourse, but of something else which the soul of either evidently desires and cannot tell, and of which she has only a dark and doubtful presentiment.

If Hephaestus, son of Zeus, were to ask the pair: "Do you desire to be wholly one, always day and night to be in one another's company? For if this is what you desire, I am ready to melt you into one and let you grow together, so that being two you shall become one, and after your death in the world beyond you will still be one departed soul instead of two—I ask whether this is what you lovingly desire?"—and there is not a man or woman of them who, when they heard the proposal, would not acknowledge that this melting into one another, this becoming one instead of two, was the very expression of their ancient need. And the reason is that human nature was originally one and we were a whole, and the desire and pursuit of the whole is called love.

Myth exists as a means of conveying truths too mysterious and complex for ordinary language. The Plato legend depicts a spiritual reality of deep significance to all men and women, one that holds the key to their fulfillment. The twin-soul concept illumines the true nature of love and indeed perhaps the purpose of the soul on earth.

The soul craves completion and return to its creative source. It is our belief that the way of return is first through the spiritual development of the individual, as far as is possible in the divided state, then the union of the soul with its missing half, its twin, and then a reuniting with the group souls from which it separated long before.

The Cosmic Design

The picture of creation is one of division and reunion. Let us follow the design for the birth of souls.

In recurring cycles Father-Mother God pours itself forth into manifestation, later to return the perfected creation to itself. Through the interactions of its masculine and feminine principles, it begins the division of its one spirit into the many. In this first birth is established the pattern for the later divisions of the ovum-sperm into the many cells of the human embryo. The cosmic law "As above, so below" is here demonstrated.

In a continuous process of division, the divine energy descends into form. Throughout the universe, groups emerge, each group harboring a multitude of souls-to-be. These are the "cells" of the "body" of God, and each is a life in itself.

The group souls separate into ever smaller units. As the groups separate, each of them is endowed with its own characteristics. The smaller the groups, the more closely the souls within them cohere. They memorize one another, even in the dim prebirth state. The longer the association, the more indelible will be the memory. By this memory they will find their way back to one another in the time of ascent, locating their own group, returning in the order of their coming. Inherent in the separation is the reunion. The transcendent mind stands above, willing the completion of itself.

The desire for return will infuse every atom of life through the long journey back to the unity of its beginning. Even in the throes of division, the newly forming lives will yearn for the oneness from which they came. With the birth of souls comes the birth of loneliness. This is the first consciousness of pain, and it will lead to the human realization that all pain is in separation, all joy is in union.

But the separation does come to an end. As the groups divide into their smallest configurations, there emerges a host of single soul-units. These are unformed souls. They are still only potential. Aeons must pass before they evolve to human state, yet they are whole in themselves, masculine and feminine together, containing all their unrealized potential.

Seemingly alone in the universe, filled with longing for the soul families from which they have been cut adrift, these entities must suffer yet another loss. There is a last, fateful division: each is struck in two, their masculine and feminine forces gathering into equal halves. Yet each retains the seed of the other, creating the polarity that will bring about the ultimate reunion.

This final severance completes the descent, where-after the law of attraction begins the reassembling of the whole. The soul at last has a clear direction: toward the lost half of the self. The divided soul must now evolve through all the lower forms of nature on its way to being human. Throughout the world of nature, and then through the human world, male and female seek each other ceaselessly. Evolution is spurred as we are drawn toward the goal of reunion and toward the summit of return.

When sufficiently evolved as human beings, we will be ready for the twin meeting. At that stage we will come into contact with some of our group souls. The group souls, or soul mates, are encountered before and after the twin reunion. There is a general in-gathering, as a response to the call from above.

The group reunions, having begun on earth, continue after death in the world of spirit. Group will join with group in recognition and boundless joy. All across the universe they will be drawn together by the thread of memory. It is a memory of bliss, the Source bliss, unconsciously perceived by unformed souls. The completed souls will return to the Source in full consciousness as perfected beings, creators in their own right, expanding the consciousness of God. That is the purpose of all our struggle on the ascent.

At the summit is perfected love, every created soul loving every other. The foundation is the love of men and women. Whenever people meet in love exchange, there is an ascension of their souls. When twin souls reunite, the ascendance is jet propelled. The twins join the God-force that draws all life upward. They are more than the sum of two; they are three. As Plato puts it in the *Symposium:* "The original human nature was not like the present, but different. The sexes were not two as they are now, but originally three in number; there was man, woman, and the union of the two." From this came the name *Androgyn.*

In reuniting after their long journey, the twin souls will become androgynous once more. Close as they will be when they find each other on this earth, their one soul will still be inhabiting two bodies. They will grow in oneness increasingly as they scale the heights of spiritual existence in the afterworld. Yet they will forever retain their individual natures within the unified soul. Always there will be communication between them, love exchange and creative interaction at levels of consciousness and bliss beyond our imagining.

Certain spiritual writings confirm the eternal principle. The following comes from the sacred literature of Sufism, an ascetic and mystical Islamic movement that first appeared in Persia in the eighth century:

Out of the original unity of being there is a fragmentation and dispersal of beings, the last stage being the splitting of one soul into two. And consequently love is the search by each half for the other half on earth or in heaven, a search that can become desperate. . . .

As twin souls are so alike to start with, it seems necessary for them to go their different ways before they can complete each other. Identity and complementarity are the two driving forces and axes of love. . . . For the complete being there must be a blending of the two.

This is to say that an individual must be strong in identity before being able to complement the twin. When the twins meet, their complementarities are not entirely fulfilled but open to further advance. The two have achieved sufficient security within themselves that they are not dependent on another for a sense of self. Then they are ready to recognize the other, to stand with the other, and to surmount the inevitable conflicts that arise in the course of human relationships.

Twin souls have been described in another way by the late Bulgarian master Omraam Mikhaël Aïvanhov, writing in the 1960s in *Love and Sexuality,* part one:

Every human being possesses a sister soul. When man leaped like a flame, a spark, from the bosom of his Creator, he was two in one and each of his two halves was the perfect complement of the other; each was the identical twin of the other. Later, these two halves became separated, each of them taking a different direction and evolving in its own way. During the course of their evolution they sometimes meet and, if they recognize each other, it is because each carries the image of the other in the depths of his being; each has put his seal on the other. Every human being, therefore, carries the portrait of his sister soul within him; it may be a very hazy image, but it is there, and this is why every man and woman comes to earth with a vague hope of finding a soul who will fulfil all his needs and with whom he may be united in total harmony.

Sister souls are everything to each other; no other being in the world can fulfil them in the same way. This means, therefore, that all those you have ever encountered since the very first of your many incarnations, all your husbands and wives, all your lovers or mistresses, have left you because they were not for you. You may have been together for a while, but only for a while, like a pot with a lid that doesn't fit. Whereas two souls that God has created together fit each other, nothing can tear them apart and they have no fear of being separated. When one of the members of a married couple is afraid of their partner being lured away from them (and, as we all know, there is no reason why this should not happen), it is a sign that that partner is not really the beloved sister soul. A woman loves a man and he goes off with another woman; a man loves a woman and she leaves him for someone else . . . But sister souls can never do that; they recognize each other with absolute certainty and never abandon each other.

When such glory awaits every one of us, we might wonder why the principle of twinsoulship is so little known. We can only deduce that we have not been ready for it. Knowledge is given in the time of readiness. Perhaps the twin-soul plan could not be made known on a broad scale until we were established in this new age of Aquarius. Humanity may have had to evolve to a point where it could make right use of this marvelous news. We believe that point has been reached and that great numbers of incarnated souls are able to love unconditionally and thereby find and rejoin their lost halves.

Where then is our true beloved, our twin soul, and how shall we find each other? The twin may be very near, awaiting the last steps in growth, which both must take to be ready for reunion. Readiness is everything. The meeting can take place only after the point of arrival has been achieved within ourselves. Though we cannot predict it, the time is known by the universal forces that have been guiding us toward each other for aeons past.

Who could have known of the threads extending infinitely back in the lives of Johanna, a painter, and Philip, a book designer and illustrator? Johanna and Philip met informally at an art gallery one summer evening. They were strangers to each other and attending the function at the gallery with different motivations: she because it was the opening of her exhibition, he for reasons unknown to himself; he had merely followed an inner impulse.

Johanna was uncomfortable in social situations, and though she was the focal point of the evening, she stayed in the background. At one point she found herself behind a group of people looking at one of her paintings. One man made a deprecatory remark. Suddenly another spoke up in fiery defense of the work, informing the critic that he had missed the essence of the picture. Johanna listened, spellbound, as he spoke of its soul dimensions. Though enormously excited and pleased, she also felt self-conscious and afraid of being noticed. As the viewers began moving away, she turned and left the room.

Johanna took refuge in the coatroom, berating herself as she had so often done for this need to separate herself. There she lingered awhile, struggling with her impulse to take her coat and go home.

A man entered, walking absently toward his jacket. He looked up. It was he, the man who had spoken on her behalf. Johanna stepped toward him.

"Thank you," she said, "for defending my painting." She added, smiling, "I wanted to put my arms around you!" There was a moment's pause; then she astonished herself. "I think I will!" And she flung her arms about him.

He returned her strong embrace for an instant before she broke away, laughing, unembarrassed, though she had never in her life opened her arms to a stranger. Normally it would have been all she could do to put out her hand. Philip introduced himself, and they began to talk there among the empty coats. Both were loners with few close friends and had a haunting sense of inadequacy on that account.

Johanna had often suffered from a certain "conversational claustrophobia." She felt pinned like a butterfly by the small talk with which people entertained one another. Her mind longed for reciprocal exchange, but this seldom happened. Unable to participate in exchanging social niceties, she withdrew into herself and her work. Though she longed for love, she withheld herself from love with her prickly persona and her blunt way of expressing herself. She had been hurt in her relationships with men and now carried her defensive shield as protection. Like the mythical princess, she could only be freed by love; yet love had not been able to find its way through.

Philip handled social encounters by taking the stance of the vigilant observer. His directness in defending Johanna's painting had been uncharacteristic. Kind and sensitive to others, he rarely lashed out as Johanna did. Though as their friendship grew, he would come to value her bluntness. She on her part would admire his restraint.

Philip's self-control had deep roots. Like Johanna, he was successful in his career and presented a strong front to the world. Inwardly he suffered from feelings of inferiority, which made him defer to others less gifted. His neurotic complex had placed a ceiling on his growth. He had tried to break through it, but his ceiling, like Johanna's shield, would not yield to force but only to loving recognition.

Philip had struck the chord of recognition in perceiving the soul-essence of Johanna's painting. The same echoing familiarity sounded in her with her sudden embrace and the opening of her heart in friendship. This was a soul contact, a recognition of the soul-self in the other.

The love that grew between them was not from a new seed but was a flowering of that which had always been. It unfolded as simply and quietly as a spring garden. Johanna recalled the comfort of their long first talk. "I felt so at home with him. Being with him was as easy as being with myself—yet better!"

Though both had stood apart from the social mix where conversation too often seemed empty and meaningless, they had both longed for authentic communication. Together at last, the floodgates opened. They talked endlessly, roaming the countryside, navigating busy streets, or sharing the quiet of the nights. Thoughts flew; their minds ignited new insights; they were carried along on the same creative joy that they both received from their work.

The twin is the mirror likeness, the other side of self. Yet so marvelous is the plan of God that when we find the twin we find a unique and fascinating individual. Part of the fascination no doubt lies in the fact that we are seeing an essential part of ourselves reflected in new light. But also, the separate paths taken by the divided souls have brought different experiences to each—different but complementary. The other of our soul is ever new, ever interesting, bringing to us what we lack, have been wanting, and are ready to receive. We complete each other, not in an instant but through a new process of growth, becoming a closer part of each other, yet miraculously becoming more and more unique in ourselves.

The paradox of twinsoulship is that two become as one and yet, in so doing, increase their individuality. In

twin-soul unity we never become bored but are held in
the fascination of perpetual growth.

In twinsoulship, close attention is paid to the being
of the other. Abraham Maslow, in his study of the love
relations between spiritually aware people in *Toward a
Psychology of Being*, describes this as B-cognition:

> In B-cognition, the experience or the object is fully
> attended to, having become for the moment the
> whole of Being. Since the whole of Being is being
> perceived, all those laws obtain which would hold
> if the whole of the cosmos could be encompassed
> at once. . . .
>
> Concrete perceiving of the whole of the object
> implies also that it is seen with "care" . . . with the
> sustained attention, the repeated examination that
> is so necessary for perception of all aspects of
> the object. The caring minuteness with which a
> mother will gaze upon her infant again and again,
> or the lover at his beloved, of the connoisseur at
> his painting, will surely produce a more complete
> perception than the usual casual rubricizing which
> passes illegitimately for perception. We may expect
> richness of detail and a many-sided awareness of
> the object from this kind of absorbed, fascinated,
> fully attending cognition.

The eye of the soul holds the vision of the perfected being. Each twin, in gazing at its opposite, can

glimpse that perfection and, through the power of love, help it to manifest.

Something of this was at work with Philip and Johanna. Both had been blocked by a gender imbalance. Philip's overdeveloped feminine or yin sensitivity, turned inward to feelings of inadequacy, had restricted his basic masculine or yang self. Johanna with her forbidding manner had given negative expression to her yang force, inhibiting her true feminine nature. She had feared her feminine softness, but through the alchemy of the twin-soul relationship, she discovered that in her softness lay her strength. It was revealed not as weakness but as creative openness, receptivity, the very basis for profound and reciprocal love.

Johanna was one who never cried, carrying old griefs and unshed tears buried deeply inside. Philip's acceptance of her was complete, his love unconditional. He encouraged her expressiveness, and in opening to Philip's influence, she allowed herself to release long-buried tears.

Gently he probed the painful areas of her past. "Cry!" he would say when he sensed grief rising in her. Taking her in his arms, he urged over and over, "Cry! Cry to your heart's content!"

She gained understanding of him as he too revealed himself in depth. And as the expressive, tender, and generous soul aspect of her yin was nourished, she became in turn the instrument of his liberation. Her understanding of Philip's true being allowed him to grow nearer to his proper stature. His inhibiting self-doubts began to fall away as his innate male powers were identified, appreciated, and repeatedly affirmed.

Writes Maslow: "Repeated, fascinated experiencing of a face that we love or a painting that we admire makes us like it more, and permits us to see more and more of it in various senses."

This he calls "intra-object richness." We could speak of intra-person richness in each of this twin pair as they perceived the highest and finest in each other, and the fullness of their hearts gave expression to the perception. This served to aid their gender balancing and show us that the twin-soul meeting may bring psychological help that has been needed and not found elsewhere. If the will for growth is strong, the two can be drawn together and, through love and mutual assistance, bring about the necessary changes. Even after the twin-soul reunion, the inner work will continue. The twins' contributions to each other's growth will be their most rewarding acts of love.

We see this mutual reinforcement in their exchange of letters. Philip writes to Johanna:

For the first time in my life I feel complete, and solidly content and happy with what I am. This is so largely because of what you have recognized within me and nourished in me. I'm so appreciative and grateful for your ever-present and unwavering love. How uplifted I feel to be so much beloved by such an elevated soul as you! The more I recognize in you, and I do, progressively, the more I become myself.

This brings to mind the image that in our twinship we are like two trees that stand apart but close together; we have roots that dig deep in common soil and obtain nutrition from it, the common soil being our earthly experience, our immersion in society and in our genetic background. Our trunks extend straight upward, side by side but separately, and our branches intertwine as we exchange with each other and nourish each other; our leaves are extended upward into the stratosphere, to welcome the sun and its energies, receiving from it and spreading forth our own emanations, higher and higher as we ascend. Our growth is in terms of our mutual nourishment. Our trunks grow as we stand in close proximity and exercise our deep perception of each other; while our branches intertwine.

In another letter to Johanna concerning the nature of true love, which is the love of the soul, Philip attempts to explain:

When we speak together, as you know, we have a deep communion. That is contact soul to soul. It's very different from gazing romantically into each other's eyes. It's a meeting in a more mysterious region, yet it's very real, very deep. It's much beyond language; it's communication that's almost telepathic, like the kind of thing I imagine is true in the upper realms where there is no language, but there is nevertheless the transmission of knowing. That is soul to soul, and it's an accompaniment of love: there are ways of love that go along with that. I know that I feel them in my heart and solar plexus.

This describes very well the new region that is entered with the twin union. It is truly a meeting of souls in a dimension far beyond the physical. Soul love pours down through all the levels of being, illumining the mind, purifying the emotions, engaging the body in sacred sexuality.

There is a new consciousness, a greater closeness to God, the origin of the love. In returning to each other, the twin souls aid the whole in returning to the Source. They become keenly aware of responsibility—the responsibility inherent in all higher life to contribute to the upliftment of the rest. This is why we see so many twin souls joining their forces in works of service—

conducting growth workshops, writing books, teaching in many ways. They are following their bliss and beckoning to others.

Because they have touched new levels of inspiration, twins can perhaps be forgiven the excesses of language that often mark their communications to each other. This occurs most vividly among poets, as we will see in chapter 8 in the love letters of Carl Sandburg. Their emotions are larger than human emotions; they are spiritual feelings and can't be expressed in ordinary words. It is not that twin souls take off into the ether. Their love is firmly grounded, but the depth of their bond enables them to reach so high.

The realm of the soul is a magical realm to our everyday eyes, though perfectly natural to those who abide there: mystics, lovers, children, and angels. This may explain why the twin meetings so often have a magical touch in the sense of happenings beyond the ordinary. Johanna and Philip's meeting is an example. Such turns of fate could result from intensified activity by the higher forces that are continually guiding separated souls along the path to union.

The great sweep of cosmic design beginning with separations beyond number reaches its first culmination in the repairing of the individual soul. All the forces of the universe reverberate to this climactic event. It is the moment of arrival and of reward for the two individuals who have long worked toward it.

Johanna and Philip had each striven for personal evolution impelled by a soul-knowledge of the need to realize their completion as individuals. Only when that was achieved were the matching halves drawn into each other's orbit to form the completed whole.

It could almost be said that the twin appears on the scene when least needed, when each half-soul has reached its highest point of independence in the divided state. This is also the pinnacle of aloneness. Every man and every woman must climb the mountain alone, able to stand firm against the high winds that buffet the elevated soul. It is then, out of the mist, that the twin appears, not in response to emotional need but to fulfill the deepest need of the soul. By the marvelous design of the Divine Planner, the ultimate loneliness of the spirit gives way to the first great joining and the end of loneliness forever.

This is not like the fall into love. Falling in love generally means that one person becomes lost in the other, abdicating the self and entrusting it to the heart of the beloved. The twin-soul reunion is a descent into the depths of the true self, the dwelling place of the soul.

Following her first few conversations with Philip,

Johanna mused in astonishment, "I'm on the edge of falling in love!" That night she had a telling dream:

> I am walking across a narrow footbridge, and it
> begins to soften all along one edge. I realize I'm
> going to fall. I look down and see that the fall will
> be far, and I'm afraid I'll be hurt. Then a voice
> says, "Don't fall! Jump!" The bridge gives way; I
> jump and my body remains upright. I'm aware of
> angelic hands softly beneath me, breaking my fall
> and guiding me all the way down into what proves
> to be a great depth. I land lightly on my feet and
> find I'm holding a book. I open it and discover it
> is the story of my life.

Fear of extinction, of self-loss, runs deep in human nature, accounting for the terror of death in those who see death as the end. Throughout life, conflict between oneself and others provides the polarity against which the soul struggles on its upward journey. The bridge in Johanna's dream is the bridge that connects twin souls wherever they may be. When the union with the twin is achieved, self and other become one; the bridge collapses. Nevertheless, even at this level the ancient fear of self-loss casts its shadow.

Johanna, interpreting her dream, describes the jump off the bridge as a necessary leap of faith, entrusting herself wholly to the other and thereby coming into possession of herself. The book that she holds on landing tells of her life in its completion.

The twin-soul union reflects in miniature the ultimate union of all souls with the Source. As below, so will it be above. The one is given at the level of our understanding as an indication of the other that is far beyond it.

Helena Blavatsky, founder of the Theosophy movement, writes in *The Secret Doctrine* of reabsorption as

> *absolute existence,* an unconditioned unity, or a state,
> to describe which human language is absolutely
> and hopelessly inadequate. . . . The human mind
> cannot, in its present state of development, reach
> this plane of thought. It totters here, on the brink
> of incomprehensible Absoluteness and Eternity.
>
> Nor is individuality lost because absorbed. . . .
> Once reached, the same Self will re-emerge as a
> still higher being, on a far higher plane, to recom-
> mence its cycle of perfected activity on the day
> when the Great Law calls all things back into action.

The concept may be beyond our grasp, but it is given us to taste the bliss of those higher states right here on earth. Who has not experienced it at moments? Certainly the peak moments of sexual union, that window into the world of spirit, are among them.

From bliss we came, every human being springing

from the passing bliss of another, and to bliss we will return. It is the reason for everything; it is the substance of everything.

The Maharishi, at the start of his Western ministry, sat one evening cross-legged on a sofa, a tiny figure on an immense stage in an almost empty Albert Hall in London. Holding a flower in his hand, he waited peacefully until the few dozen people who had come to hear him fell silent. Then he laughed and said, "Life is bliss."

Life is bliss for him because he is awakened. It will be so for all of us, since our purpose in being is to attain full consciousness and bliss. We awaken through love. Without love we would sleepwalk forever.

We live in a universal network of love that is urging us awake at all times. An almighty act of love produced the division of souls and the design for their return to each other through increase of love. The joy of the twin reunion is great, but it pales before the raptures that will attend the reassembling of the group souls, each composed of united twins. Progressively the groups will be added to one another, expanding in dimension as the teeming clusters gather throughout the cosmos, multitudinous as the stars, each soul within them expanding in order to contain the bliss.

Every action of our lives is a move toward love and union; some are more direct than others, that is all.

"God writes straight with crooked lines," the folk saying goes. As we evolve we learn to straighten out the lines.

The straightening doesn't always happen on this planetary level. A young couple in their early twenties were married in 1940 and were romantically in love. Ten years later love had turned into its opposite. Two children were caught in the vortex. The divorce made headlines because of a vicious custody battle that brought out the worst in both parents. The judge separated the children (Solomon style), assigning one to each parent. And so two children grew up, each with an embittered parent who would scarcely allow the other parent's name to be mentioned in the home.

Forty years later the wife heard through her daughter that her ex-husband had died. Sometime afterward he came to her in a dream.

> This was a lucid dream, the kind I have come to believe is a real spiritual experience. He was bending over me—and I will never forget my astonishment at seeing again the handsome, dark-haired young man I had fallen in love with so long ago. I know that in the world of spirit we can choose to appear at any age we desire. The skin of his face was satin-smooth; I wanted to stroke it to feel its silkiness. As I did so, I realized that it was the light substance of the spirit body.

But his appearance was the least of it. The greater thing was that he was speaking to me with immense love and tenderness. There was forgiveness, and a plea for my forgiveness. We were back in the love that we used to feel. I realized it had not been extinguished. I awoke in that mood of love, knowing we had been truly reconciled.

I wrote to both my daughters and told them of the harmony that now existed between their parents. It brought tears to my eyes to be able to say at last the words they must have ached to hear: "Love from Mother and Daddy."

It was clear to her that in the afterlife the soul of her husband had assumed its true nature. He had viewed her soul in perspective and been able to see their departure from love as necessary paths of learning for them both. Because she had cultivated her spiritual faculties, she was open and receptive to this psychic contact.

This was not a twin-soul marriage; yet the marriage was subject to the universal pattern of division and return in enrichment. Wherever love splits apart it will increase and return. It can go nowhere without meeting itself.

In whatever circumstance love divides, it will reunite, following the law of all things. A family splits up over money. Others say, "What a shame." God smiles. He is taking them further afield, guiding their growth in the direction of love and reunion. It is the only direction; there is no other. They will be reconciled, if not on this earthly plane, then on the next.

On the way, there is bound to be suffering. It will be outgrown. The masters affirm that we evolve through suffering until we learn to evolve through joy.

The twin union is the security of evolution through joy. The crooked lines begin to straighten out. They straighten progressively until finally it is "back to God as the crow flies."

At the great return, the purpose of all the divisions will be seen: the evolution of souls from the first divine spark to the splendor of full being, adding themselves to Father-Mother God in all their individual glory.

Twin souls, each returned to the androgynous union, will forever retain the two unique identities, masculine and feminine, which they evolved in the dim past, two within the one, as the one remains one within the many.

The Masculine and the Feminine

MASCULINE AND FEMININE ARE THE EVER-
creative, self-perpetuating energies of God manifesting throughout the universe. These are described in
The Synthesis of Yoga, by Sri Aurobindo, one of the
greatest of spiritual masters, who, with his partner-
guru, the Mother, founded the now-famous ashram at
Pondicherry, India, in the 1920s.

> The masculine is the infinite Godhead who con-
> tains all things in a potentiality of existence. The
> feminine is his Shakti, the same Godhead put
> forth as a self-aware force that carries all within
> her and is charged to manifest it in universal Time
> and Space. She is the World-Mother, creatrix of
> the universe, putting forth the gods and the worlds
> and all things and existences out of her spirit sub-
> stance. . . . She is the mediatrix between the eter-
> nal One and the manifested Many. By the play
> of the energies which she brings from the One,

she manifests the multiple Divine in the universe, evolving its endless appearance out of her revealing substance. By the reascending current of the same energies, she leads back all towards that from which they have issued, so that the soul in its evolutionary manifestation may more and more return towards the Divinity.

And so the pattern for the individual soul is set in motion as the Deity divides and returns. All souls perfectly repeat the duality of God, the two-in-one, separated and returning.

We can understand our masculine and feminine natures and the twinship of our souls by studying the twinship of the masculine and feminine within God. Each of us is a microcosm of the macrocosm. Once we understand the nature of the universe, we possess a master key by which we may unlock all the mysteries of our own souls.

Aurobindo speaks on the opposite aspects of the Creator in terms that apply perfectly to twin souls:

They [the masculine and feminine of God] are the two poles of existence in one Being. . . . They represent two different sides of itself, obverse and reverse in relation to each other. . . . The two lines or currents of their energy, negative and positive, effect the manifestation of all that is within it. Even

in his activity he holds in himself all her force and
energies ready for projection; even in the drive of
her action she carries with her all his observing
and mandatory consciousness as the whole support and sense of her creative purpose.

In just this way the male twin contains the energy
of the female, while she is supported from within by
his creative power.

The twin souls were assigned their native gender at
the moment of division, yet the two halves were never
fully separate, for each retained the seed of the other.
Evolution has seen the slow growth of that seed within
each half of the soul, the growth always directed toward the time of reunion. That time comes when the
dual energies in male and female achieve an exact balance as they are balanced in the Divine.

We are masculine and feminine beings at core, de-
scendants of the Eternal Feminine and Eternal Masculine. We are sexual beings; our sexuality is built into the
blueprint of creation. It cannot be denied. It leads to
the love that is rooted in the soul. Twin-soul love,
therefore, is destined for everyone. It is for you; it is for
me; it is for the rich and the poorest of the poor, for the
prisoner in his cell, for the old and abandoned, for all
who pine in loneliness.

Every soul hungers for its completion; every life

tends toward that. Though hidden in depths, the urge for completion is the motive from which all motives spring; it is the drive for return to that which was lost.

First was the loss of our original home in God. Next was the loss of our oppositely sexed self. From the center of our severed soul, we hear the call to return, but we can only return in wholeness of being. We must reach laterally, to the other of ourself; then we can turn upward to the greater completion.

We live in a time of gender confusion, even gender denial. We must look more deeply to the source of our sexuality. Sexuality is soul deep. Through all our incarnations we have been developing our basic gender while nurturing the essence of the opposite in our male or female soul. We have assumed myriad forms in our lives on earth, passing through the lower kingdoms to the human, the masculine soul seeking its perfection in a succession of male bodies, and the feminine in a succession of female bodies.

Our evolution has been single-focused in purpose: to return us to ourselves at an advanced stage of completion. Unswervingly we have followed the distant aim of becoming woman, becoming man, becoming whole.

It is often said that we alternate our sexual forms in our successive incarnations because the soul needs the experience of both sexes. But this does not take into account the twin-soul principle, by which the female half of the soul evolves the yin and the other the yang, each harboring the essence of the other, never changing gender. During our successive lives we have been evolving our basic gender self as well as the contra-gender within.

Through the experience of each sex, the male consciousness enters the female soul, and every development of the feminine nature is absorbed by the masculine counterpart. They learn of each other by becoming built into each other, as once they were.

It is for growth into consciousness and experience in material form that they are parted and then rejoined. They have no need to alternate their sexes in earthly life. As they evolve into self-definition she could say, "I, woman, know what it is to be a man, without need of the body parts; I know it as my own inner masculine takes on strength and fortitude, creative initiative and leadership." He could say, "I, man, have knowledge of womanliness, as my womanliness expands my heart from within, inspires my higher mind, and stirs my most compassionate and tender feelings toward the young and the needful all about me."

When at last they find each other, they are able to reestablish their oneness because they have become one in developed soul-substance. The part of the male that has grown to completion in the female soul is a part of her being, as is the extension of herself residing in him. This explains why Cathy, in *Wuthering Heights,* can say in truth, "I *am* Heathcliff!"

She is he and he is she. Yet she is a whole woman, and he is a whole man. What is it, then, to be a woman? What is it to be a man? The answer is to be found in our understanding of the two divine energies interacting within the human soul. Man is not one thing and woman another; but yang energy is one thing and yin another. They combine differently with different proportions in the soul of man than in the soul of woman.

In Eastern philosophy yang and yin are defined as follows: yang is the initiating impulse, which divides and delineates; yin is the responsive impulse, which nurtures and reunites. Without yang nothing would come into being; without yin all that comes into being would die. Yang is mental activity in its forceful aspect, yin the imaginative and poetic exalting the merely mental to the beautiful. Yang goes ahead with things, yin contains things within herself. Yang does, yin is. Yang in masculine givingness bestows the gifts; yin in feminine being receives, preserves, enhances, and redistributes them.

Yang constructs, yin instructs; yang implements, yin complements; yang is strength, yin is endurance; yang is knowledge, yin is the mystery that reveals itself and becomes knowledge. Yang is the discoverer, yin lures toward greater discovery. Yang is the self-developer, inspired by yin, the self-dedicator, for her development and his dedication. Yang is the lover and therefore beloved; yin is the beloved and the source of love. Yang is will and yin is wisdom, and one without the other is neither, and together they are joy. Yang is as the day turning into night, and yin is as the night preceding the day; the one is the force that drives the waves of the ocean forward, the other the force that draws them back so that they may go forward again.

To be a woman or a man, therefore, is to stand on the ground of our gendered self with our complementary opposite gender in proper balance. This opposite gender we call the contra-gender, meaning the feminine component within the man and the masculine in the woman. Man is yang-based with yin rising. Woman is yin-based with yang rising. The balances and proportions are the measure of their spiritual maturity and gender strength. The twin union can occur only between a man complete and secure in his manhood and a woman confirmed in her womanhood. A truly strong woman is strong and happy in her femininity and comfortable in her secondary masculine character; a fully masculine man exhibits all the best of his yang qualities along with yin sensitivities in high degree. This is the condition for what Maslow calls self-actualization. When a self-actualized man and self-actualized woman meet and bond, their gender characteristics are shared, flowing in harmonious exchange.

Male and female energies do not become homogeneous. Separate and distinct, they can be recognized at work within us, and recognizing them, we can employ them creatively, bringing them into balance and hastening our progress toward the completing union. That balance will be different for every soul. It is achieved partly by nature's efforts and partly by our own. We are in creative partnership with the God-force in our work of reassembling and reuniting.

You are a woman? Somewhere there is a man working to bring your womanly powers to fruition within him: when you meet you will recognize yourself. You carry in yourself, like a forming child, the very qualities of maleness that define his essence.

You are a man? Your complementary opposite is growing in the direction of your maleness, developing in herself the unique character of your yang strengths. They will reflect back to you in the delight of recognition when at last you encounter each other. The exquisite harmony that will exist between you will result from that understanding between the two parts of you that are the same. You have never ceased to live and grow, one within the other.

Aurobindo writes of the feminine and masculine duality of God: "This Duality, though separate in aspect, is inseparable. Wherever there is one, there is the other."

Physicists have recently discovered, and were astounded to note, that if a twirl in one electron of a two-electron atom is reversed by external force, the electron twirl of the other is similarly reversed, despite the vastness of the distance between.

This parallels the nature of the twin-soul duality. The twins are "separate in aspect"; that is, they occupy two different forms, but wherever there is one, the influence of the other exists in the spiritual dimension. Every action in the course of their evolution affects the soul of the other by a natural law, which has become manifest on the material level.

The development of yin-in-yang and yang-in-yin is evident in the sweep of history, as we trace our growth from primitive man and woman to the evolved partners of today ready to join in twinship. Early man was all yang, but for the germ of the feminine deep within. Early female was all yin, submissive and dependent. From them we derived the cliché "Women are passive, men are aggressive."

Woman can be wholly passive still, when the shadow influence has her in its grip. But in its developed state, passivity—that which takes in, gestates, nurtures, brings to birth—becomes receptivity. Receptive passivity provides a clear channel for the intuition, the direct line to God and creativity itself. It is the yin energy of the eternal feminine, and it is not for woman to treasure alone but to share with man. Similarly, the aggressiveness of early man, or man in the shadow, transmutes to creative initiative as he grows into his full stature and is revealed in light. The creative power of the eternal masculine in woman is employed in her unique way, giving energy and strength to her creations, then flowing back to him refined and beautified.

This gender balancing is the condition of true equality, the kind that need not be fought for; it is built into the soul, needing only to come to recognition and maturity. Such distinctions are necessary before the sexes can understand each other. It is the negative force in the psyche that binds us to stereotypical thinking which breeds hostility where there should be love.

Ultimately the yin and yang polarities will exert their magnetic force and bridge the gap between every pair of twins. Mutual recognition, now a rarity, will become common. Such a recognition story between psychologist Ken Wilber and Treya Killam is told in his book *Grace and Grit.* Both were spiritual seekers; Ken was an author of many books on spirituality and consciousness.

We quote from an entry in Treya's journal on the night they met in 1983.

At one point we all went into the kitchen for some tea. Ken put his arm around me. I felt a little uncomfortable since I hardly knew him, but slowly I put my arm around him. Then something moved me to put my other arm around him too and I closed my eyes. I felt something indescribable then. A warmth, a kind of merging, a sense of fitting together, of blending, of being completely one. I let myself float with it for a moment, then opened my eyes, surprised.

What had just happened? Some kind of recognition, a recognition beyond this present world. It had nothing to do with how many words we'd shared. It was spooky, eerie, a once-in-a-lifetime feeling. When I finally left at 4:00 A.M. Ken held me before I got in my car. He said he was surprised, he felt like he never wanted to let me go. That was just how I felt, like I belonged in some almost esoteric sense in his arms.

Ken describes drifting into sleep that night, "only to awaken with a start: I've found her. That's all I kept thinking: I've found her." Then in the morning he describes the following:

As I lay in bed, I noticed a series of subtle energy currents running through my body, which felt very much like the so-called kundalini energy, which,

in Eastern religions, is said to be the energy of
spiritual awakening, an energy that lies dormant,
asleep, until aroused by an appropriate person or
event. . . . Incredibly, the same thing was happening
to Treya, and at exactly the same time.

And from Treya's journal:

Fascinating lying in bed this morning. Feeling
little wavelets of vibration, very clear and distinct.
Sensations in my arms and legs, but mostly localized in the lower half of my trunk. What is happening when this goes on? Are things loosening
up, held tensions from the past dissolving?

I focused on my heart, felt an opening very,
very clearly, from thinking of that sensation I had
with Ken last night. An amazing powerful surge
from my heart, that then goes down into the center
of my body, and then up toward the top of my
head. So pleasurable and blissful it's almost painful, like an ache, a longing, a reaching out, a wanting, a desire, an openness, a vulnerability. Like how
I would feel perhaps all the time if I weren't protected, if I dropped my defenses . . . and yet it feels
wonderful, I love the feeling, it feels alive and very
real, full of energy and warmth. Jolts my inner
core alive.

This energy that Treya describes is the magnetic
energy constantly playing upon us beyond our con-

sciousness. It is the incipient bliss of the cosmos and is activated by soul union: twin souls, group souls, the meditator's union with God.

Masculine and feminine found their ideal balance in Ken and Treya. Treya wrote: "Within two weeks of our first meeting we decided to get married. It was fast. But somehow we both seemed to know, almost right away." The strength of their twin-soul union would fortify them through the years of heartbreak that lay ahead. Their marriage was one of enormous trial and reward, as they battled for five years with the cancer that finally claimed Treya at age forty-one.

The language of twinship appears throughout their communications, as with Ken's flowers to Treya on the eve of her mastectomy and his note: "To the other half of my soul." And he provides us with a fine description of their gender harmony. They are in Germany, seeking yet another treatment for the rapidly metastasizing cancer; Ken climbs a hill on the city limits to reach a high fortress, where he has these thoughts:

> From the top of this tower I could see for perhaps a hundred miles in all directions. I looked up: Heaven; I looked down: Earth. And that's what started me thinking of Treya. In the past few years she had returned to her roots in the Earth, to her love of nature, to the body, to her femininity, to her grounded openness and trust and caring.

While I had remained where I wanted to be, where I myself am at home—in Heaven, which, in mythology, does not mean the world of Spirit but the Apollonian world of ideas, of logic, of concepts and symbols. Heaven is of the mind, Earth is of the body. I took feelings and related them to ideas; Treya took ideas and related them to feelings. I moved from the particular to the universal; Treya moved from the universal to the concrete. I loved thinking, she loved making. I loved culture, she loved nature. I shut the window so I could hear Bach; she turned off Bach so she could hear the birds.

In traditions, Spirit is found neither in Heaven nor in Earth, but in the Heart. The Heart has always been seen as the union point of Heaven and Earth. Neither Heaven nor Earth alone could capture Spirit; only the balance of the two found in the Heart could lead to the secret door beyond death and mortality and pain.

And that is what Treya had done for me; that is what we had done for each other: pointed the way to the Heart. When we were first together, we were sometimes irritated by our differences. But we soon came to see that that was the entire point, that we were different, and that, far from being whole and self-contained people, we were each half-people, one of Heaven one of Earth, and that was exactly as we should be. Together, joined in the Heart, we were whole; we could find that primal unity which neither alone could manage.

Gender harmony between two people occurs after individuals have labored to bring their own interior forces into balance. This is illustrated in the following story about Diane.

Diane had despaired of ever finding a man with whom she could have a fully loving relationship. She was in her late thirties, extremely attractive and dynamic, with a colorful personality. She had devoted many years to establishing and running her own firm in the media field, and she now ranked among those at the top. She termed herself a feminist, and most of her close friendships were with women. In her kitchen she had a bulletin board with a collection of cartoons disparaging the male sex. Though a source of amusement, the bulletin board was also an indication of her confused feelings.

Diane had been involved in a seven-year love affair with Anthony, a Frenchman. Their relationship was fraught with conflicts, but these were submerged in the waters of the ocean that separated them. The vast distance that lay between them stirred their longings; the letters that flew back and forth were filled with passionate declarations of love. However, their differences rose quickly on the occasions when they visited each other.

Diane discovered that whenever she stayed at Anthony's apartment in the small village where he lived, a remarkable change came over her. She would suddenly be overtaken by a fit of domesticity—cooking, cleaning, beating rugs on the balcony rail alongside other housewives. Part of her wondered what on earth she was doing, yet she could not deny that she was enjoying herself.

In truth she was expressing her most basic nest-building instinct, her yin nature. This feminine base had been neglected in her years of competing in the professional world. Her yang forces had been in the forefront and created an imbalance of the complementary feminine energies within her. Her feminine nature was literally starving.

In Anthony's apartment the pendulum swung the other way, and yin was claiming its own. But when the swings are very wide, they always create a new imbalance. Her days of domestic bliss among Anthony's pots and pans always ended in disappointment, for Anthony, too, was out of kilter on his gender scales. He was ahead in his feminine growth and behind in his masculine. Diane's burgeoning feminine demanded a strong masculine partner to complement and complete it.

The yin and yang forces work differently in the

man and in the woman. In realized womanhood, yin
energy is demonstrated as active-receptive, creative in
the highest sense, the pure receptor for the spiritual in-
flow. In the less-developed woman it is displayed as
neediness and a clinging to the male. In the undevel-
oped male, yin tends toward passivity and weakness,
while in the fully matured male it expresses itself as
tenderness, empathy, and nurturing. These qualities
shine with true luminosity in the man with evolved
masculine power.

These qualities are what Diane sought and could
not find in Anthony. His passivity and lack of masculine responsiveness roused her anger and finally her
contempt. The unraveling of the relationship was long
and painful, leaving both of them bewildered, despair-
ing, and full of blame.

Diane employed her active yang strength to seek recovery and healing. A devout Catholic, she embarked
on an intense spiritual search. Aided by her long habit
of prayer, she courageously investigated her own psyche.

Central to Diane's awakened perception was the
sense of her feminine nature, her love nature, which for
so long had been stifled, then contorted in its struggle
to come into alignment with her masculine side. Diane
saw that she and Anthony had initially been attracted
to each other because of their strong polarities. Diane's
masculine self was in the forefront of her personality,

and Anthony was dominated by his feminine self. These are the opposites that attract, then repel, for they are not the complements.

True identity for Diane would only come when the forces of her feminine gender assumed supremacy over her contra-gender. The same would hold for Anthony. Diane had been hurt in love many times before and realized that she had been suppressing her feminine nature out of fear—fear of being vulnerable and the hurt it can bring.

In order to clear psychological blocks from her past, she sought counseling. In her loves, she found, there were echoes of her ambivalent love relationship with her father. Through the help of counseling, meditation, and introspection, Diane perceived this and gained the courage to expose herself, step by step, to new ways of relating. The antimale cartoons were thrown away. Her business had always been an expression both of her talent and of her flight from her femininity and spiritual longings. She reduced the intensity of her involvement in it. She reordered her priorities, downscaling her material needs to enable her to spend hours each day on her yoga practice. She branched into service to the sick and stressed. Through intensive reading and prayer she rediscovered her relationship with Christ. As time passed her soul became more nearly balanced. She recounts:

In my busy-ness, I had ignored my real thirst for
the spiritual, in relating to God and to others. As
soon as I had made the decision that God was my
priority, my life turned around. I found myself in
Paris at a conference to promote awareness between the Eastern European countries, Russia
and the West. The Archbishop of the Russian
Orthodox Church was a keynote speaker. There
was no logical business reason for attending, but
my heart wanted to go. I met a man there who had
also come from the other side of the world and for
the same reason. Sam was a business entrepreneur/
arts promoter. We had a lot in common. He had
a wonderful mind, and a full understanding of
human dilemmas. His clarity of thought and his
expansive heart were a rare combination. Sam lived
in a city not too far away from me. We kept in
touch by phone and letters, and I found myself
opening to him more and more, becoming intimate. I was ecstatic one day when we shared our
favorite prayers by fax! We shared our thoughts on
God, on emotions and feelings, and all the time I
felt held in a light net of love. We visited each
other frequently. I had never been so close to anyone. I felt safe in the knowledge that we were there
unconditionally for each other on our spiritual
journey. It was a time of great happiness. My life
had taken on a soft golden glow of love and possibility, of hope, and of the miraculous.

Once again Diane had become involved with a man at a distance while seeking emotional intimacy. Though Sam was much stronger in his masculine being than Anthony had been, and Diane more secure in her feminine, she was to find that a gender imbalance remained. There were fears and uncertainties in Sam that came to the fore as the relationship intensified. His feminine was still in a stage of dependency. He and Diane were unequal despite their compatibilities and strong soul connection.

Diane had fallen deeply in love, having dared at last to surrender and make herself vulnerable, risking the long-anticipated hurt. Interpreting Sam's resistance as complete rejection, she fell into despair. Heartbreak consumed her. She had been so certain that theirs was a deep and abiding love, the true love of the soul. She had felt the soul-love spreading its radiance through all her being in her newfound connection with her spiritual source.

After the storm of suffering had abated, she discovered that she had not been entirely wrong. Sam remained steadfast in friendship, reaffirming his genuine feelings for her. Their love had changed course but still ran deep. Though not twin souls, they were close group souls, commonly referred to as soul mates. In his unwavering devotion and support, Sam confirmed the strength that Diane had first seen in him. She felt certain that they would be lifelong friends, consciously bonded at soul level and contributing to each other's spiritual growth.

Diane didn't doubt that her long troubled love affair with Anthony had been a preparation for the greater learning that would come to her through Sam. And her relationship with Sam had been necessary for her to realize that she needed to do more inner work in mind, body, and spirit.

It was not until several years had passed that she met Mark at a dinner arranged for singles interested in spirituality. She immediately felt a connection with him. It was not his outward appearance that drew her but his sensitivity and open interest in discussing spiritual subjects with her. When they went out for the first time, they found they both were rereading *Does God Exist?* by Hans Küng, a spiritual classic. Along with the soul response, the similarities of their experiences pointed toward twinship.

- They had both run their own communications companies and had recently shifted to careers of service.

- They had both undergone therapy to clear up past psychological problems and blocks, to make them more aware and conscious of themselves. They therefore had the words to express their emotions and what they were feeling.

- They had both been celibate for two years, preparing their bodies for the fulfilling and tantric sexual relationship they both desired.
- They both had a daily spiritual practice of prayer and meditation, and both were involved in some community work.
- Their ethics and sense of the moral were compatible, as were their priorities toward their families and friends and their work.
- They were both involved in some physical activity—she in yoga and he in running marathons.
- They were both vegetarians.
- They both had the same religious upbringing and background.

So Diane and Mark's mind-body and spirit were in a profound embrace. This was not a romantic love that happened suddenly; it was a slow unfolding of two souls who had searched their lives for the other and finally found completion. To be supported entirely for herself was a new feeling for Diane.

When they came together physically it was to satisfy a thirst for a union much larger and deeper than a sexual one. Lovemaking for them was as natural an act as speaking, sleeping, and being. Their sharing increased, and each now exclaims that they have finally found all that they wanted in another, and more. The bliss and joy of their encounters, sexual as well as in the everyday, are imbued with wonder and respect. They both acknowledge that it is God who has guided them to each other; and it is God to whom they offer their future lives. Married now, they are stronger, clearer, happier, and more peaceful beyond anything they've ever known.

They recognize that the path toward the twin is often a painful and difficult one, as it was for them. Though each had many disappointments, their faith was their guiding light. In their personal growth to a deeper understanding of the self, their difficult experiences had not hardened them but had opened them to the possibilities of a healed heart.

We approach the twin through our learning in our experiences of love. The lessons may be learned in love partnerships or through simply developing love capabilities in ourselves. Our general relatedness to others is the broad canvas of our labors. Like a painter, we work all over its height and breadth.

When we remain open, all experience is used by

the soul for self-discovery and identity, pointing us in the direction of authentic selfhood and thus toward union.

⌒

The psychiatrist's office is a place in which the work of self-discovery and gender balance is carried on intensely, often reaching dramatic heights. Coauthor Maurie Pressman cites the following case of a young man being treated for depression:

> My patient Roger was about to give up on everything. For too long he had been afraid of asserting himself; instead he was overly accommodating, dependent on the approval of everyone with whom he worked. All this "niceness" became a straightjacket reinforcing his feminine self, which preferred to be loved and taken care of, at the expense of his assertiveness and his innate leadership qualities. He had long felt overshadowed by his father, and evidence kept accumulating that he was inwardly enraged. Finally I ventured an interpretation, suggesting that he might be holding on to all of this fear and helplessness and hopelessness in order to subdue his rage, which in fact was the other side of his strength. I handed him a pillow and suggested that he beat it to allow the rage to surface. After some protest he finally started to strike the pillow

and began to feel some anger. I encouraged him further, and he felt more anger. I told him to bite the pillow, and he began to bite it and shake it like an animal.

Surrendering to the full power of his rage, he began to roar, his face contorting to that of a demon—he confronted me with it, his eyes closed. His rage went on for some time. When it subsided, he curled into a fetal position and began to suck his thumb.

This young man illustrated the release from gender inhibition to gender development, and then to gender balance. The release of his "demonic" energy, which arose from the same source as his assertive strength, was also the release of his masculinity. He told me that in the course of his exercise with the pillow he had even felt sexual stirrings.

One day he came in looking crestfallen. He had just chaired a staff meeting during which his associates had severely criticized some of his professional plans. It seemed to me he had reverted to the old pattern—trying to lead them by gaining love instead of asserting his authentic self and his position. I asked, "Have you forgotten your power? Have you become afraid of your 'demonic' energy?" He returned and confronted his associates, presenting again his original plan. Though it was not adopted, he sensed a new respect among them.

At about the same time he began to see a young woman for whom he experienced love and a strong sexual drive. Sexual relations followed; he told me just how much pleasure he felt when he was able to embrace her and express his protective strength.

As Roger released his aggressive energy in a sublimated healthy way, his masculine self grew stronger. He came more and more into his own, becoming more spontaneous and more physically relaxed. A gender balance was established that had not been in evidence before. This development did not entail any loss of his yin sensitivity or of his affection for the people who were important in his life.

It may be thought that gender is an inborn thing—only that it is fixed, genetic, unchangeable. But Roger teaches us something more. Our gender may be inborn, but it must be developed and nourished by our own efforts. In order to develop his basic gender identity, Roger had to be willing to challenge deep-seated fears. The aggressive energy thus released was used to cultivate himself.

His was a refined use of aggressive energy, which when sublimated becomes assertion. This has nothing to do with the shadow side of the self, which would otherwise express itself as cruelty or self-seeking power.

And so, beneath everything, the defining and balancing of gender forces goes on. It is the work of the soul and the means of restoring the divided soul to itself.

"Why can't a woman be more like a man?" Professor Higgins mourns in *My Fair Lady*. That is what a woman is doing in the pursuit of her completion. Her masculine force asserts itself, sometimes taking the lead, as it seeks its true balance within her. She becomes more like a man, then consolidates her new powers and becomes the woman she is.

Masculine identity has been following the same process. This is the goal toward which the conflict of the sexes has been moving. The long gender struggle, we believe, has been preparing the way for the union of twin souls on a broad scale.

Harmony and equality are not yet won. The outcome is certain, however, as certain as the dual love-nature of God. As our eyes and our souls open to this fact, we move closer to the joy on the other side of the struggle.

Ken communicates this joy, writing of his and Treya's marriage:

> Our favorite activity was still very simple: sitting on the sofa, our arms around each other, feeling the dancing energies in our bodies. So often we were taken beyond ourselves to that place where

death is a stranger and love alone shines, where
souls unite for all eternity and a single embrace
lights up the spheres—the simplest way to discover
that God most definitely is embodied, love of the
two-armed form.

But their simple happiness was short lived, for they
inherited, in Ken's words, "four months of happiness
and five years of hell." They were to touch the depths of
darkness, even turning in fury on each other as they
rose and sank beneath the weight of the challenge they
had been given.

Yet Treya died in bliss, in a manner that evokes the
deaths of saints, certain in the knowledge of their oneness with each other and with the universe. One intuits,
reading their illuminating story, that they had accepted their burden of pain and suffering for reasons
beyond their own soul advancement. It was their gift of
service. Treya's writings on cancer and illness reached
an estimated one million people around the world.
She cofounded the Cancer Support Community in San
Francisco and personally counseled hundreds of cancer patients.

In the memorable story of their love, *Grace and Grit,*
they do not shrink from taking us into the blackest
depths of their human weakness—making all the more
exalting the triumph of the bittersweet finale.

I put Treya in bed that evening and sat down
next to her. She had become almost ecstatic. "I'm
going, I can't believe it, I'm going, I'm so happy,
I'm so happy, I'm so happy." Like a mantra of final
release, she kept repeating, "I'm so happy."

"You promise you'll find me?" she asked.

"I promise."

"Forever and forever?"

"Forever and forever."

"Then I can go. I can't believe it. I'm so happy.
This has been much harder than I ever thought. It's
been so hard. Honey, it's been so hard. . . . But now
I can go. I'm so happy. I love you so much. I'm so
happy."

During the last two weeks, Treya had been almost obsessively going over what I had said to her
on the way to our wedding ceremony, five years
earlier. I had whispered in her ear, "Where have
you been? I've been searching for you for lifetimes.
I finally found you. I had to slay dragons to find
you, you know. And if anything happens, I will
find you again."

We had kept each other going, and became
each other's teacher during those last extraordinary
months. My continued service to Treya generated
in her almost overwhelming feelings of gratitude
and kindness, and the love she had for me in return
began to saturate my being. I became completely

full because of Treya. It was as if we were mutually generating in each other the enlightened compassion that we had both studied for so long. I felt like years, maybe lifetimes, of karma was being burned out of me in my continued response to her needs. And in her love and compassion for me, Treya also became completely full. There were no empty places in her soul, no corners left untouched by love, not a shadow in her heart.

At the end, Treya made a gesture, trying to say something to me. "You're the greatest man I've ever known," she whispered. . . . "My champion . . ." she kept repeating it. "My champion."

I leaned forward to tell her that she was the only really enlightened person I had ever known. That enlightenment made sense to me because of her. That a universe that had produced Treya was a sacred universe. That God existed because of her. All these things went through my mind. All these things I wanted to say. I knew she was aware how I felt, but my throat had closed in on itself; I couldn't speak; I wasn't crying, I just couldn't speak. I croaked out only, "I'll find you, honey, I will . . ."

Treya closed her eyes, and for all purposes, she never opened them again.

Will Ken have found her? Without a doubt. When one twin dies, the two are parted only on the physical plane. The soul, indivisible, simply awaits the passing over of its earthbound half and its ascension to the next stage of experience.

Twin Souls in Conflict

THE SUFI TEXT STATES: "REMEMBER [TWINSOUL-ship] is a gift, carrying with it the tremendous responsibility of being able to face up to the greatest challenge to which any two human beings could be subjected, and whereby they are graced."

The movement of all life is toward reunion of its separated parts. In human life that movement becomes a pull in two directions: toward the need of the self and toward the need for closeness with others. The conflict between self and other is a central dilemma of the human soul. In resolving it, that greatest of challenges is overcome.

Although self-need and other-need appear to be in conflict, they actually represent the two aspects of our growth, much like the alternating movement of our legs as we walk. Our task is to keep the two sides of ourselves in balance, giving each its due and continuing to move ahead.

We can gain a picture of this balanced flow by studying its action in the lives of twin souls. The action is by no means always smooth. But, by the law of their nature, twin souls cannot be parted and so are compelled to resolve their conflicts in the quickest possible way. We can learn from them to do the same, for *the twin soul model is an ideal for all human relationships. As we study it and make ourselves ready, we lead ourselves and others into this path of ascension.*

The Sufi symbol for twin souls is that of two interlocking rings that cannot be pulled apart. The two complete rings signify two individuals, whole in themselves, though interdependent within the larger whole. The great challenge for twin souls is to join in the spiritual heights, where they are one, and to bridge those heights with their life together on earth, where they meet as separate human beings. If destined to join their lives in a close physical relationship, they find that normal conflicts arise. They are twin souls, not twin persons. They have different psychological backgrounds, a body of divergent influences, habit patterns, and expectations. Emotional adjustments are required, as with any couple.

But their conflicts are solved in a special way. These rings allow us to visualize the process:

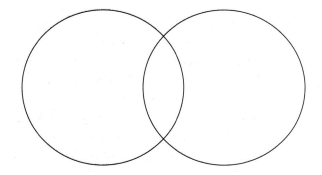

The rings depict two souls with an overlapping area of commonality. Their shared ground, the area where the rings overlap, represents the part of the twins' natures that is identical; the open areas on either side represent their individual selves with their unique characteristics. The rings are not static but fluid, shifting back and forth as the twins relate to each other. There is a widening or narrowing of the central area and of the spaces on each side, where the two selves hold apart, displaying minds and wills of their own.

When the twin souls experience conflict, the rings move apart—but only so far. By the law of their nature they cannot completely break apart. They are drawn together again by love, the action of the Mother, to whose heart they are now closer than ever, and by the unbearable pain of separation.

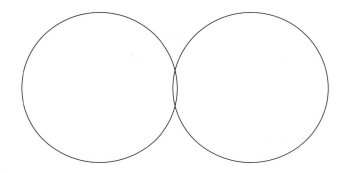

Emotional conflict is hard for anyone to bear; for twin souls it is unendurable. Being so much a part of each other, they feel the other's hurt ever more keenly. One heart breaks for the other. They must end the other's pain in order to heal it in themselves. The emotional dynamics of the twin soul never allow the feeling "let him suffer."

Twin souls are obliged to seek resolution, and quickly. Guided from soul-levels, they act together on a basis of complete honesty. Laying aside pride and ego, they summon the courage to face their own truths and relentlessly seek the root of the problem. Nothing is left unaddressed, nothing is concealed or distorted to partial truths. They permit no residue of anger or hurt to remain and weaken the fabric of their relationship. Instead their relationship is strengthened by differences. As they return after a clash, love surges in them anew. They flow toward oneness to their limit while retaining, as they always will, their individual selves.

Conflict will arise over and over again; it is part of the cycle of nature, and of the growth process. With each cycle, twin-soul love is strengthened. Growth is twofold: they grow closer in oneness, and together grow upward. Gradually the conflicts become fewer, and their growth centers around their inner work, each aided by the other.

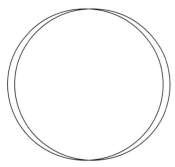

Twin souls have karmas that are intertwined throughout eternity. In living apart, twins have been accumulating and working through their karma in preparation for their coming together. As to the individual karmic debts brought to the union, they will help each other discharge them, just as the burden of monetary debt is shouldered together in a good marriage. Similarly they will share the joy of each other's karmic credits. The inexplicable happiness that falls over the one may stem directly from the past deeds of the other.

Remember that throughout their long journey of return, whatever happened to one had its reverberations in the other, much as occurs to lesser degrees between every created soul in the universe. Twin souls are responsible for each other in a way that is closer, though not different, from the manner in which we are all responsible for one another. At root there is no such thing as separate karma, only degrees of the joy or pain that follow from our choices.

Proof of twinship accumulates through the process of retreat and return, as symbolized by the interlocking rings. As the twin souls find that they do not break apart, indeed cannot, their bond passes through the stages of alchemical purification. Faith permeates their consciousness—faith in themselves, in each other, and in the universe. In this way they are graced.

Inevitably there will be conditions of stress between certain twins, causing temporary disruption of their life circumstance. Twin souls can live on opposite sides of the world and continue in oneness of being. The two rings can stretch infinitely without breaking. Twin souls are called upon to meet every kind of conflict. We saw how Treya and Ken were tested to the very iron of their souls.

Two more twin histories give us further examples.

One demonstrates a severe test, and the other shows a union with almost no conflict.

Rebecca is a transformational therapist. She describes the arrival of her twin in this way:

> Several years ago I awoke in the middle of the night. Hovering about eight or ten inches above me as I lay in bed was the face of a man, his gaze soft yet intense and full of love. Even in the darkness, I could see him distinctly, and realized that this was his astral or ethereal presence. Although the visitation seemed peaceful, there was at the same time an urgency about it—he seemed to want something from me. As I lay there, aware of his presence, I began to feel an enormous love for him.
>
> I couldn't remember his name, but I knew who he was. We had met at a workshop seven years earlier in California, and were paired up for a brief exercise. The assignment was simply to look silently into the other person's eyes for a few minutes and to be aware of any feelings that might arise. When the exercise ended, a short break was announced. During the break, he invited me for a walk along the bay.
>
> "While I was looking into your eyes," he said, "I remembered my mother, dying in my arms. Although she had never showed me much love, on that occasion suddenly I could *feel* how much she

loved me. The love I felt for you during our exercise was like that, but even stronger."

His words resonated in some deep place within me. I felt much love for him, though I did not say so. Silently I thought, I will always be with you.

Throughout the days following the nighttime visitation, I felt his presence almost constantly. Wherever I went, he seemed to be with me, and my heart expanded with more and more love. Soon, to my great surprise, I began to fantasize that we were lovers.

My marriage had ended some years before. I had remained celibate since then, unwilling to compromise either my work or my integrity in a relationship that would be less than what I wanted. With this sudden and unexpected visitation I wondered, "Am I just desperately lonely and not even aware of it? Am I making this up?"

The experience continued, notwithstanding any of my rationalizations. About a week later, during my early-morning meditation, I remembered his name: Clayton Gibbs.

Locating his phone number through a person who had attended that seminar, I called him. The sound of his voice on his answering machine brought back an even more vivid memory of our bayside walk years before. I felt a surge of excitement as I left a message.

The following day, as I conducted a workshop, I felt and "saw" Clayton walking around the room, working with me. At night, I dialed his number in California again. This time he answered. We talked for more than an hour. I learned that his marriage had ended the same year mine had. While I was raising my daughter alone, he had finished raising his four children. There were many other synchronicities in our lives—events that made it appear we had been traveling in tandem, though miles apart.

Two months later I flew to California for a week and we met several times. I felt my overpowering love for him expand even more, and sensed the same from him. I spent a good part of that week surrendering my will to God's. Though I wanted a personal relationship with Clayton, even more important to me was the need to be aligned in every way with God's will for my life. I was accustomed to living alone and focusing my energies on my work. I desired a relationship with Clayton, but did not *need* a relationship.

Yet it seemed that a relationship was God's will. Clayton, who had been a successful businessman, had recently begun searching for a way to turn his humanitarian and business skills to a spiritual purpose. When he came to see me in Colorado, a month later he felt impelled to join me in my work, and I welcomed him eagerly. We began living together and giving transformational workshops together, with an emphasis on promoting harmony within couples. People said that as a pair we were inspirational.

Our own harmony astonished us. There were so many similarities. We shared the same likes, dislikes, tendencies and idiosyncrasies, food preferences, types of weather, sleep patterns.

Our sexual life was wonderful. When we consummated our union, both of us had been without partners for some time. Clayton, who had once been very sexually active, said that with me it was almost as if he were a virgin. "I've never felt anything like it," he said. "I'm having to learn all over again."

Then, from this great height of happiness, it all began to go wrong. The conflicts started in small ways, causing us pain and shock, and then escalated swiftly. We fought. Clayton had been a millionaire and now felt the lesser half of the pair delivering seminars. I was a strong woman and at times he found me very bossy. He was going to have to leave, he said, and reassert himself and his manhood.

I was devastated, I knew I could not carry on this work without Clayton. Nor could I live without him now.

In desperation, Rebecca and Clayton sought psychiatric counseling. Clayton realized that his mother's inability to express her love for him had left him with a kind of pit deep within himself, into which he feared he would fall if he allowed himself to be vulnerable in a relationship. His love for Rebecca had returned him to the earliest period of life, when he had been emotionally abandoned. At the same time her controlling tendencies excited his warrior self. Feeling combative, he wrenched himself away.

Rebecca, too, had childhood difficulties that had remained unresolved. She remembered vividly being sexually molested by a family friend when she was ten years old. When she told her parents, they made light of it, leaving her with a feeling that she must fend for herself. She did so by developing a strong male side. As counseling proceeded, she grew to realize that she had been unreceptive to Clayton's masculine protectiveness, and that the cause lay in her childhood experiences. She had been too competitive, with too much emphasis on her masculine force.

The crisis in their lives proved to be a healing crisis. Despite the gravity of the conflict, the interlocking rings prevented a rift, their mutual bond leading them into a position of greater closeness, and they resumed their work together. As teachers of transformational healing they were enriched by courageously confronting their own pain and undergoing the process of transformation themselves. Their union was fortified, and their gender forces brought into balance.

Rebecca reports now:

> I'm indulging in a luxury that I have never had before in my life, and that is the pleasure of just being female. My male side is just as strong and available, but now it doesn't have to be on duty all the time. Clayton is willing and eager to accept that role. We find it's an exact inverse ratio: to the extent that I allow my femininity, he is empowered in his maleness. I've learned that a woman must own her femininity before she can own her masculinity—and conversely with the man. We feel that the distinctions in the gender balance are so very important and we continue to work on them.

While we can expect major conflict such as Clayton and Rebecca's to appear in the lives of twin souls, we can also expect to see pairings in which harmony is the rule. In such cases we can deduce that the challenges to soul growth have been met at an earlier time.

Coauthor Patricia Joudry relates the episode of such a pair as it was revealed when she was talking to an acquaintance, Shirley, about the twin-soul concept.

"Are twin souls something like soul mates?" Shirley

asked. I answered that they were, explaining also that we have many soul mates but only one twin soul.

"Well, I'm really interested in that," she said, and confided, "you see, I have a new relationship—and it's something I can hardly believe! I know he's my soul mate, or twin soul, because we're so alike. All our attitudes and values, our likes and dislikes, our whole viewpoint on life—they're just the same. I never thought I'd meet anybody like him," she continued, her face aglow. Her happiness could scarcely be contained. "My husband died two years ago, and I was prepared to spend the rest of my life alone. Len and I have been together for a year and haven't had a single argument or difference of opinion. It overwhelms me. He's everything I ever wanted."

I then asked a leading question. "Where you are different, do you find that you complement each other?"

"Yes!" she exclaimed. "That's it exactly! For instance, I'm hyper and Len is very calm. He calms me down, and I lift him up. I'm an extrovert and he's an introvert. I draw him out—and he brings me more into myself. We seem to balance each other."

She and Len had both raised families while living two streets away from each other for twelve years. (The lives of twin souls often run parallel like this. They may pass by each other, taking no notice, until the designated moment.) Said Shirley: "My son even visited Len and his wife. Once I went over there with a message from home. I met Len. He just looked like any ordinary man to me. I had no idea of what he was going to mean to me. But it wasn't the time."

Both had had unsatisfactory marriages. They had married young and grown apart from their mates—toward their future twin (though this was unknown to them). Len's marriage broke up at the same time that Shirley was widowed. A year later they found each other.

Shirley spoke of their samenesses and complementary differences. They were both readers; both loved the out-of-doors; they were fond of art and had reproductions of the same artist's work in their homes. They loved to garden—she growing flowers, he vegetables. Shirley works in a store, and Len is a market gardener.

She goes on, "We help each other in all ways but allow each other to be ourselves—we never try to take control or change the other one. We never hurt each other; we show tenderness and care. Any misunderstandings we straighten out right away. I'm so happy!" she exclaimed many times. "We keep saying how lucky we are to have found each other. 'You're so good,' I tell him. 'If am,' he says, 'it's because of you.'"

Another similarity lies in their love of children. Says Shirley: "I told Len one day, 'Our life is so perfect—the only thing we haven't got is babies.' But he has infant grandchildren living nearby. The next day he arrived with two of them in his arms. 'Here are your babies,' he said. I hugged them to me. We love them like our own."

While the babies satisfied Shirley's nurturing, feminine needs, she was balanced with her inner masculine, the force that leads. This was shown by her taking the first step in the love affair. She tells of their meeting shortly before Valentine's Day. "I was very attracted to him. But I knew he was hesitant about getting involved after the disappointment of his marriage. So I decided to reach out. I sent him a Valentine, and wrote, 'I'd like to get to know you better,' including my phone number. He called right away! And we were off."

Such twin-soul relationships are happening more frequently as women develop their yang power and initiative, and men develop the tender qualities of their nurturant side, much treasured by a woman in a man. All over the world the assertion of women's powers and the emergent spirituality in men are leading toward the joining of twins.

Even the clash between the sexes is part of the heightened move toward resolution. If we look at conflict as it occurs between twin souls, their symbolic rings driven apart temporarily, then caught at the place of interlocking and thrown back on each other, we can see that the same design is playing itself out on the world stage. The collective soul of women and the collective soul of men are twins. They are two halves of one spiritual body, complementing each other, seeking their commonality, spurred on and inspired by their differences. Like the twins, they cannot separate, nor can they stagnate in their point of furthest difference. The only possible move is back toward union. The requirement for that move is the working through of yin and yang gender balance within and between individuals.

Shirley and Len's love experience, while illustrating again the main attributes of twinsoulship, lets us know that twin souls are meeting in every walkway of life. The great body of the world's work, the evolution of the world, is carried on by ordinary people growing in love, serving in their homes, in stores, in all manner of mundane and inglorious jobs. We needn't look for glamour in the circumstances of the twin-soul reunion. In twin-soul joinings the soul contacts the true source of glamour, the spiritual light.

This is the light that has drawn them toward each other throughout the many lives of their search. In the course of those lives they have surely met before, making incomplete connection each time. The completion that we speak of here is the culmination of a long gradual process through which their knowledge of each other has evolved. The final meeting is the one that connects them on all levels of being. It is probable that before completing themselves, and completing their lives on earth, they have had to share experiences together on each of those levels.

The master Omraam Mikhaël Aïvanhov writes in *Love and Sexuality,* part one: "A human being meets his twin soul twelve times during his incarnations on earth." He adds that sometimes the twin meeting has brought about their deaths, as with Romeo and Juliet, because "the conditions of our existence do not permit the realization of such a perfect love, such absolute love."

Yet the conditions of life on earth have been changing. The climate is now right for the meetings and the final completion of a great many twin pairs. This doesn't mean that some pairs have not experienced true union in the past. We believe that twin-soul completions will have occurred many times. As every stage of life flows into another, we have to assume that twins have been meeting through the ages, living their twinship, without knowing its name.

Why does it matter that we name it now and understand all we can of the principle? Because we have grown in consciousness, and it is time to experience our joy at higher levels of awareness.

To be happy and know that we are happy is to

receive fully the gift of humanness. To suffer and know that we suffer empowers us to transcend our suffering. Such was the basis of ancient Greek tragedy. Because the tragic hero had clear consciousness of his suffering, he became ennobled. Thus the audience was purged, uplifted, and ennobled in turn.

There is a nobility in conscious joy, for it partakes of the Divine. We open ourselves to the gift of the spirit, which will expand us finally into vessels of pure givingness. This we have been striving for in our long growth to realized twinship.

Twin Souls after Death

What happens when twin souls depart this world? Will they have to come back? We believe that by the time the twin union has been completed, the individuals will have reached a high level of spiritual development, and that they will not be obliged to return again to this earth.

Death is not only a transition, it is in a sense a reward. Ancient wisdom teaches that after death there is a time of residence in the Devachan, a period of rest. In this rest all of one's dreams are fulfilled. Then if more work is needed for soul advancement, there is return to incarnation.

Since existence on the higher planes after death is a state of bliss, it takes a special dedication to choose reincarnation. But there are those who do. They have achieved a level of mastery and yet will return in order to serve suffering humanity, and thus hasten the advancement of other human souls.

Whether twins return and return together is their choice. They might decide to come back and find each other again. They might incarnate simultaneously but live far apart, yet carry on a joint work of service. Perhaps they will meet in the evening of their lives, and greet each other in soul remembrance.

One twin might incarnate alone, to be guided and inspired by the other in spirit. This person would not be searching any longer for the twin soul but would be dedicated to the work they had jointly selected. The person would marry only if the spiritual life of the twins could benefit by it. This would be an advanced soul, developed in love, whose earthly life would be marked by true love-expression. That could include family life, public life, or a solitary life of devotion and dedication to service.

One thing is certain. The completed twins are now firmly caught up in the process that Teilhard de Chardin has described as "the hand of God gathering us back to himself."

The grip of that hand never loosens. And so the twin souls will be together forever in the infinite ways of the Divine.

Preparing for the Twin

WHEN ARE WE READY TO MEET OUR TWIN? HOW can we prepare? Before we can unite as twin souls and become whole, we must attain a relative wholeness and completeness in ourselves. The smaller completion mirrors the larger. The soul has divided but has formed into two bodies, two rounded personalities, two minds that at some level think as one yet are capable of strong, independent thought. We meet as clearly defined individuals, advanced in self-sufficiency and purposeful living. We need to be fulfilled in ourselves, capable of living alone without feelings of loneliness or inadequacy. Then we are ready for the swift advance that follows the twin union, able to stand apart, not leaning, yet giving each other strong support.

Content within ourselves, we have passed beyond neediness while recognizing our soul-need for the other. We need to be at a place where we are satisfied with our lives yet continue to urge ourselves forward. The inner urge is known as the divine discontent and is quite unlike dissatisfaction. We will have gone a long way toward resolving our emotional problems and will have learned forgiveness for what has been unforgivable in ourselves. We need to learn to love and accept ourselves for what we are while striving ceaselessly for self-improvement.

In most cases we will not be casting about for our lifework but will be firmly set on our lifepath, running parallel, similar but complementary with the life of our twin. We will have been exercising our powers and following the course set by the soul. We will possess self-discipline. We will not waste time, having learned the value of time and our own value as citizens of the world.

To the best of our abilities we will have brought our gender forces into balance, in preparation for the rapport with the complementary energies of the twin. And we must remember that the energies of the one are influencing the other all the time, so that every effort of one twin is a gain for the other. We have been reaching for each other and drawing closer by reaching for the best in ourselves.

The most important part of our preparation is inner growth. We find each other not by scanning the horizon but by turning the searchlight inward and doing the needed work in self-development.

How can we help ourselves to become such people, ready for our twin?

1. We can resolve to cultivate our inner joy, something we all possess, hidden in our depth. Joy is our true nature, always present beneath the false coverings. The reach for the true self will help us to realize that we are whole beings, capable of finding satisfaction in our lives with or without the help of another.

2. We can accept our material "things" as they are, without feeling that we will never be happy until we have a better car, better clothes, a redecorated home, and so on. We can loosen our grip on materiality, realizing that a new possession brings pleasure for only a short time, whereas every step in knowledge and consciousness is a lasting gain.

3. We can cultivate a discipline that will open us to our spiritual selves. This could be meditation, yoga, tai chi, study under a spiritual teacher, or attendance at some of the many growth seminars now available.

4. We can work toward finding our lifepath and developing our God-given talents, honoring our gifts in whatever directions they lie. Spiritual advancement is the same whether our lifework be our profession or work that we do in our spare time. Our greatest talent may find expression within the home, in raising secure children and building a happy family.

5. We can care for our bodies, respecting them, listening to them, purifying them through clean habits, good food, exercise, and avoidance of gluttony. We can purify our emotions by turning our feelings toward love and away from gossip or spitefulness. And we can purify our minds by avoiding the crude and the violent, by following some aesthetic pursuits and raising our thoughts to appreciation of the beauty and bounty of life.

6. We can pay attention to the images and ideas that we are exposed to, realizing that everything we take into our minds becomes a permanent part of us and reflects itself in our lives in some way. It is particularly important in this age of excessive noise to

be attentive to the sound stimuli we allow in, for the ear is the gateway to the brain and entire nervous system. The music of Mozart is food for the soul as well as the brain; loud rock music, in contrast, is now known to be responsible for widespread ear damage. Much of this can be alleviated by a program of sound therapy for the rehabilitation of the ears that includes Mozart and other classical composers. We would do well to make these our musical choices.

7. We can take the time for some involvement with nature, that great source of food for the spirit, whether it be gardening, walking in the woods, swimming in the sea, enjoying the rain, turning our face up to it and feeling the connection between earth and sky. As Emerson has said: "We cut ourselves off from nature at our peril."

8. We can find individuals or a group needing our help, whether it be tutoring students or driving those in need of transportation, passing on our talents and sharing our assets in some way. It may be working in centers for the homeless, visiting the sick, caring for neglected children; there are

hundreds of such ways to develop the soul
satisfaction of service and to grow through
contact at the level of human need.

We can also take the following practical steps to ascend in our personality as we relate to others. As the mind goes, so goes the personality. This means that as we train our minds we create a map that we follow leading to higher and higher stages of personal development. As we mature we wish to join with others but have no compulsion to join.

1. In order to complete our development and become ready for the twin, it is necessary to love the other for the person that he or she is, to love that person despite his or her failings. This we can do if we train our minds to sustain with patience and tolerance, managing the bad times that assault us, tolerating the emotions of anger, anxiety, hurt, and disappointment while at the same time keeping good sense, self-control, and logic. By conditioning and disciplining our minds we lead the way for the heart.

2. We can work to develop empathy, which comes from identifying with the other person, becoming the other person until we

can feel and understand what the other is feeling.

3. We can strive for clear communication, trying our best to understand the other and avoiding the implications of criticism.

4. We can control our aggressive needs. Aggression is a basic instinct. It is biological energy. It is expressed as rage in a small child who is frustrated. In the course of maturation, controlling mechanisms develop so that aggression can be contained and gradually converted to positive uses. These uses are expressed as energy, persistence, courage, protectiveness. How can we achieve this? First by wanting to control the self, then by acknowledging and containing our anger. We can then apply the energy of anger in useful ways: defending our truth, exercising energy of the mind in learning, as well as energy of the body in activity. We build psychological muscle by containing our anger, fear, and sadness and using them as a signal. When we are ready for the twin, there is a readiness to be patient and to control emotions so that they become benign and useful.

5. We can control our sexual energy. Sex is a
    biological energy. It is contained in the cells
    and alive throughout life even to the portal
    of death. It is the substrate of love. When
    poorly controlled, sexual energy cries for
    immediate release. This is most keenly felt
    in adolescence, when the hormonal urges
    are particularly strong and compelling. As
    the personality matures and sexual drive be-
    comes melded with love, sexual energy is
    directed toward one person and combined
    with tenderness, protectiveness, receptive-
    ness, and care. At this point the partner's
    sexual pleasure is at least as important, per-
    haps more important, than one's own. All
    of this is led by a desire in the mind to make
    it so.

When we have arrived at the point where we are
less occupied with our own happiness, and more with
the happiness of others, we are ready for the twin.
This is a time when we balance and make full use of
our gender powers. We exercise our yang forces for
self-preservation, but also for the protection of others,
and our yin forces for receptivity, empathy, and lovingness. The man uses his feminine side in appreciation of
the woman's marvelous role, the goddess role of love,

care, creativity, motherly productiveness. He can pursue aesthetic aspects of life without fearing this sensitive part of himself. The woman, in harnessing her yang energies, adds strength to her love and reveals her intuitive leadership and creative power.

All these bring us closer to the unconditional love of twinship. Love is conditional while we remain separate. The wider the separation between two people, the more conditions we attach to the love. It becomes a transaction. I have expectations of you, and you of me. If we fulfill each other's expectations, love is exchanged, but it is not real love. Conditions are added as the separation widens; and the separation always widens unless efforts are made to narrow it. When it has widened enough, the love turns into its opposite.

But when the separation is systematically narrowed, through maturity, tolerance, and understanding, love increases. The conditions become fewer until finally, in true union, there are no conditions at all: unconditional love. Twin lovers say, in effect: *It is not that I love you for your virtues and despite your faults. I love you for your faults as much as for your virtues.*

Finding the Twin

We will not all meet the twin in this lifetime; but if not in this life, then another, for we are immortal. Still we must prepare.

Each step upward in our love relationships brings us nearer the twin. If we appreciate the true immortal that we are, then all of our love relationships become preparation for the ultimate relationship and for the ultimate joining, the joining with the All in return to the Light.

To improve our skill in love relationships, we can behave *as though* we were twins with interlocking rings. Dr. Roberto Assagioli has written about the "as if" technique. Realizing that we are not yet enlightened, we can behave as if we were, and in this way steer toward enlightenment. In behaving *as if* we were twin souls, we can endeavor to prevent the rings from coming apart, catching them at the farthest point of division. Instead of nursing our hurts and retreating into isolation, we can resolve to understand our partner better and spring back quickly, compelling the resolution. Our bond will be strengthened, as it always is after clash and successful resolution. By thus improving our loves, even if we don't find the twin, we can come closer—a joy, a blessing, and a reward in itself.

We prepare for the twin not only in relationship to others but also in relationship to ourselves. The balance between self and other must be found and maintained. When alone we may succumb to feelings of loneliness; but loneliness must be tolerated and overcome before we are ready for the twin. Too often we equate solitude with loneliness. We feel that we must fill up our time with activity and with background noise, warding off the silence that would otherwise allow us to relate to our inner selves.

Loneliness is based on a false sense of separateness. It means we are feeling separated from our soul. To heal that separation, we must have periods of solitude, either while in a relationship or in between relationships. When a partnership ends, we might feel impelled to rush toward another connection in order to escape loneliness. But that time of aloneness is our best opportunity to relate to ourselves. The strong contact with our own soul will draw us into connection with the twin soul.

Prior to the twin union, there seems always to be a time of apartness. Both twins experience this, if not in their outward lives, then in the space they make around themselves in their meditations and solitude. Then finally, the two solitudes join, and the true sound is heard.

Alice Bailey evokes this in *A Treatise on White Magic:*

In solitude the rose of the soul flourishes; in solitude the divine self can speak; in solitude the faculties and the graces of the higher self can take root and blossom in the personality. In solitude also the Master can approach and impress upon the quiescent soul the knowledge that he seeks to impart, the lesson that must be learnt, the method and plan for work that the disciple must grasp. In solitude the sound is heard.

Listening to the Inner Voice

The sound heard in solitude is that of our inner voice, the small still voice of the soul. It reaches us through our intuition. The daily practice of meditation opens the channel to the intuition so that we may be guided by our own soul-wisdom.

We are in a time of spiritual awakening, but it also has its shadow side: psychic illusion. To the extent that we turn to mediums, psychics, and spirit sages presumed to be speaking through channelers, we cut ourselves off from our own sources. The inner voice is the only voice we can trust.

The best preparation for the twin is the discipline of listening inwardly. The twin will be doing the same. We are guided to the twin, and the twin to us, by the God-forces of the universe, and the God-force meets itself within us. It whispers: *This way, this way.* We have only to hear truly and follow.

⌐

Two who listened to their inner voices were Clare and Glenn. For a long time both had been following the spiritual path. During the final three years, Clare was consciously preparing herself, as she relates in their history:

> For as long as I can remember I've felt deep inside that my "other half" was out there somewhere. Having had various relationships, I got to a point where I was becoming increasingly conscious of searching for this person whom I knew I would find eventually.
>
> In the last relationship I had prior to finding my twin I knew I was not with the "right" person. I tried to explain this to my lover; that we could share some good times but that we would not be together forever. I could only tell him that *I just knew.*
>
> After that I decided it was better to be on my own than to be in a relationship that was not the ultimate connection that I yearned for. I was twenty-two years old at the time.
>
> I did not become involved in a relationship for the next three years. Once in a while I would meet a new man and find myself thinking, Oh no, I hope it's not him! I continued the personal practice of meditation that I had begun some time earlier, convinced that I was preparing. It was at a meditation seminar that I first became aware of Glenn. The course leader asked me whether I was going to attend another seminar some months later, and when I said yes she smiled and said that

Glenn would be there. I asked, "Who's Glenn?" She answered, "You'll see. I just think you should meet him."

In fact, when she first said his name, I felt a flush of embarrassment that I could not explain. It was almost as if we were already in a relationship that nobody knew about and she was revealing our "secret."

I did go to the seminar and I did see Glenn. The first time our eyes met I had to look away. I was afraid the depth of feeling would overwhelm me like a tidal wave if I looked him straight in the eye for any length of time. I was clearly not ready to deal with the intensity of the feelings that were being stirred up inside, and we barely spoke to each other.

During the next years our paths crossed several times and we began to get used to each other's presence. Looking back, I can see that this phase of "preparation" was essential. If we had gotten together right away, the power that was generated might have blown an inner fuse. I found myself thinking about Glenn more and more as the months passed. He had moved to the West Coast and was spending a year alone in an isolated house by the sea. This was part of his own preparation for what was to come.

Finally we both attended another weekend

seminar. He asked me to give him a lift in the car from the station to the center, and I was so exhilarated that I drove the wrong way for twenty minutes before either of us noticed! When we arrived, it felt almost as if we were arriving as a couple although it was clearly not yet the case. However, it was during this seminar that we reached the point of no return. It happened when the group leader told everyone to find a partner to work with. Our eyes met across the crowded room and that was it. We could no longer deny that something incredible was carrying us along, though we couldn't begin to guess where it might be leading. At the end of the seminar, although we had done no more than talk for hours, we both found parting incredibly difficult.

We started writing to each other and Glenn invited me to the Coast for a holiday. During the three weeks before the holiday, our letters became utterly intense, and we also spent hours on the telephone together. Sometimes I felt a little scared about what was happening—but above all, we both sensed that we were getting ready for something very important indeed and were going through a major initiation.

At last I arrived for my holiday—and the next phase of our life began. We found out that we complemented each other totally. Each felt that the other provided the parts that had always seemed to be missing. For the first time ever, we both felt complete.

On the first evening, Glenn asked me to marry him. I had always valued my freedom, yet I surprised myself by accepting his proposal. We both felt that we had been together many times before—and that this time we would be connecting at every level: spiritual, mental, emotional, and physical.

In contrast to other relationships our souls seemed to be intimate already, and we spent the next ten days getting to know each other's personalities. We found it strange to call each other by our given names—Glenn and Clare—as these didn't seem appropriate at the inner level where we had the real connection. So we started simply to call each other "babe"—and to this day we rarely call each other by our actual names.

. . . It seemed as though inspiration were coming through from a high source, due to the spiritual energy generated by our union. We understood that each individual is incomplete, that a part of each of us resides with the other twin and becomes manifest only in the harmonious union of the two.

All of this was seven and a half years ago. We got married one year later and since then we have loved, lived, and learned a great deal . . . but that's another story!

It has been asked, "Do twin souls have to be advanced souls?" To an extent, yes, they must be, for they have been a long while evolving toward their reunion. But every soul is more advanced and less advanced than multitudes of others. The descent from the Source was an infinitely long process. We did not all begin the ascent at once. This earth has been called the schoolroom of the universe. As a schoolhouse it contains different grades. Younger souls are in the first grade, older ones in university, ancient souls far beyond that. Twin souls will reunite at a specific stage of their evolution, a grade set by the universal laws of learning. If grade ten is a time for graduation and for twin-soul discovery, the soul would not be ready at grade three.

It should be said at once that not having met the twin doesn't signify a lack of evolution. Graduation may have occurred in a previous existence. And there will be many more beyond this school of life. We ascend through "initiations," the term used in Theosophical and other spiritual writings for the ascent of the liberated soul through the vastness of cosmic consciousness.

In assessing where we are on the continuum, we can

ask ourselves a number of questions: Do we possess optimism, faith in life, humor? Do we know joy? Have we developed our gifts? Have we developed our gender characteristics and our contra-gender qualities? Are we able to love? Do we desire to aid others?

There is one final sure test of our evolution. The less evolved person looks back at the steps already taken and is proud; the highly evolved person looks up at the heights yet to be scaled and is humble.

Obstacles to Twin-Soul Union

TWIN SOULS MUST CONQUER OBSTRUCTIONS ON the path to each other. The obstructions may come from within or without. Those from within could arise from unresolved personality problems. Obstacles from without could take many forms: a prior marriage commitment, the possessiveness of determined parents, the destructive influence of a neurotic partner, or the force of circumstances that may keep people geographically apart.

If twin souls meet and one or both are already married, there could then be a conflict between the human-made law of marriage and the spiritual law of soul attraction. But while laws made by humanity take little account of the heavenly, the spiritual laws have regard for the earthly. The divine agency that directs the movement of souls is not likely to bring twin souls together in such circumstance as to break any true moral code.

A responsible marriage partner will not abandon

responsibilities for the sake of a new love—even if the love is for a twin. In this case, the partner will feel compelled all the more to honor the needs of those to whom he or she is committed. This is the real meaning of honor, conforming to karmic law as our conscience dictates. When we hear of a man or woman walking out on dependents because the twin soul has appeared, we can be fairly sure the twinsoulship was false.

True twins, by contrast, will demonstrate that twin-soul love is expansive. It is not bound to the conventional wisdom but to the new wisdom, which sponsors growth, which expands to embrace, which urges the journey of everyone upward toward further soul meetings. Twin souls who are unable to join their lives fully will look for the purpose in this restriction. They will know that they are meeting a test. Perhaps they are called to a work of service that will be better accomplished as colleagues and loving friends than as lovers.

Twin souls are not so likely to be swept away by passion as those who are more earthbound. They will not always experience a driving need for physical intimacy. Their intimacy is of the spirit, their passion directed toward fulfilling the will of God—and their reward comes accordingly. Whatever the obstacles that spring up in their path, nothing can interfere with their soul union.

They may meet in the night on spirit levels, in dream life, and, as consciousness expands, in previously inconceivable visionary and transcendent encounters in the higher worlds. They travel to each other in their astral and mental bodies. Their mental powers and love capacities increase, with influences flowing back into their daily life and work. Deprivation spurs the higher mind and soul to vigorous exercise of their gifts. That is the compensation for their temporary separation.

Certainly it will happen at times that a twin-soul union precipitates the breakup of an existing marriage. This would be a marriage that was already collapsing under the weight of its own stresses. The collapse would be as much a part of the divine plan as the union of the twins. Letting go and uniting are integral parts of nature, and thus of human nature. In such a case the meeting of twin souls could be the stimulus to a new cycle of growth for all concerned.

When one marriage partner strays from the marriage, we can be sure the partners are not twins. The eternal triangle is a pattern that has been repeating all through history. But the triangle is not eternal; only the twosome, the right twosome, is eternal. The struggle to form the eternal twosome has occupied men and women everywhere and in all times. We have been those same men and women at lesser stages of ourselves. All the while we have been changing partners, as in an age-less dance, all moving toward the ultimate union.

Now, when the finale draws near, we can only hold the present partner with open hands, and with all the love of which we are capable. It is the music of the spheres that calls the steps, while the response of the heart beats the rhythm. When the dance is completed, no one will be left on the sidelines.

And the finale is drawing near all over the world, for the time is ripe. A great many of the obstacles to union have been overcome through our labors in past lives. Since the twin-soul marriage best serves the universal purpose, we may expect that the majority of twin souls will now find each other in circumstances that allow them to join their lives. "Those who are truly married on earth are in heaven one angel," wrote Emanuel Swedenborg, a seventeenth-century Swedish philosopher and mystic.

The truly married will gradually became the norm here on earth. Even now the enduring twin-soul marriage is becoming a reality. Its distinguishing features are fidelity, harmony, joy, love, and trust. Such a union is the realized ideal of male-female fulfillment.

We must ask ourselves what obstacles we are placing, or allowing to be placed, in the way of that fulfillment. Are we, for instance, caught up in a restrictive relationship?

Sacrificing the Self

All relationships are purposeful for growth, but they should not be allowed to turn from positive to negative effect, stunting rather than promoting growth. Such a change is a sign that growth has ceased or become drastically unequal.

In the twin-soul relationship both twins are evolving at the same pace. They move forward in step, though not in military step. One progresses in one area, the other in a different one, and each draws the other forward. They are continually advancing, carried along on a wave of mutual leadership and initiative. This applies to any strong, enduring marriage, whether of twins or not-yet-twins.

Incompatibility in marriage means a difference in the partners' direction and speed of growth. Their souls are at different stages of evolution. One partner may be outgrowing the other, outgrowing in a sense of spiritual aspiration. The demands of the other may become an impediment to the one on the spiritual path. Under those circumstances, the one must measure the responsibility to grow against the responsibility that is the contractual marriage.

This becomes a particularly difficult problem when the limited partner is one who is given to neurotic illness. Then the caretaking partner is nurturing the sick aspect of the other, to the detriment of both. It is necessary in these cases to confront the limited partner with the difficulty, even at the threat of dissolving the marriage. Very often, as addiction therapists have proven, such a threat advances the fixed partner to self-inspection and movement onto the path of recovery, and ultimately onto the path of spiritual growth.

The strong partner will not always find it easy to distinguish between caregiving and self-sacrificing. That distinction can only be made by paying close attention within. There is soul-satisfaction in giving care where care is genuinely needed. Where it is not, the soul of the giver is troubled. Unenlightened self-sacrifice impedes the advance of both personality and soul. The self is not ours to sacrifice: it is God's. The self must be free to move at God's direction.

If we are bound to a situation where outer freedom truly is not possible, we can still work toward inner liberation. In claiming our freedom to follow the voice of the soul we will be preparing for the larger, fuller life, and for the twin, through whom we enter the larger, fuller life.

Recognizing the Shadow Side

A most serious obstacle to the twin union is concealed hostility toward the opposite sex. Unrecognized mother-hatred in a man will cast its shadow over his relations with all women. Furthermore, that shadow will attract to itself the dark forces ever-present in the universe and perpetually seeking opportunity to invade the human psyche.

The aim of the antievolutionary force is to oppose the union of souls. This it does by sowing seeds of enmity in the human heart and thus obstructing the course of love. No greater obstruction could we find than the ages-long subjugation of women. Recent history has brought female fury to the surface in order that it might be dispelled. Life's purpose is always to create a positive effect, however drastic its methods might seem:

The persecution of women, like all persecution, is an expression of the dark, separative impulse. Throughout history the rage and hatred characteristic of the shadow forces has found a focus in the female sex. Those motivated by power and sadistic sexuality have made women the targets of diabolic acts. A rapist is a man possessed by a demonic entity. The My Lai massacre and the sexual atrocities committed by American soldiers in its thrall expressed the blood lust of the same dark psychic swarms that engineered the depravities of ancient Rome and the Holocaust.

The rise of feminism was a clear invitation to the powers of darkness to capitalize on all that had gone before. Women had necessarily to confront their rage, the accumulated rage of centuries. They had been victimized by forces of violence and domination, and men were the visible instruments of their suffering. Not recognizing the unseen forces at work behind such victimization, many women, in their new militancy, spread the blanket of blame over the entire male sex. Men's counteranger was stirred in reaction to feminine rage and gave birth to the men's movement. Men felt that they were being blamed for all that was wrong in the world; they proclaimed that they had become victims themselves.

There has been a swing back to center, but the perception of men as women's enemy has not been completely erased. Feminists who still retain some lingering hostility are postponing the day of their completion in love.

But all will come to realize that men are not the enemy of women. It is the enemies of humanity that have made it seem so. Men are the lovers of women. They are the twin halves of women, preparing themselves, as women are, for the great encounter.

To erase the enmity between men and women, we need to learn to recognize the existence of evil forces within ourselves and in our lives, and to take steps to counter them. It is said: "All that is necessary for the triumph of evil is for good men (and women) to do nothing." And all that is necessary for the obstruction of the light within us is to ignore the existence of darkness.

There is a shadow side to our personalities, a shadow side to society, and a shadow side to the spiritual energies around us. Before we can overcome the outside agencies of evil, we first have to recognize the way we empower them from within. Neither the forces of light nor darkness can function on this plane except through a human vehicle.

The influences that shape us in earliest childhood are those that determine our susceptibility to light or dark powers. To state it simply, the child who is loved, and so learns to love, becomes open to guidance from the spiritual forces of light. But the deprived and abused child does not easily develop into a person who loves and wants to serve others. In the child who is maltreated, the angry and sadistic component latent in us all becomes enlarged, creating an opening for forces of darkness and cruelty.

The personality makeup, then, provides the path for communion between the outer forces of light or darkness and the positive or negative tendencies in the individual.

We all fall somewhere between the extremes of the tenderly treated and the abused. There are many loving people who were abused as children and have overcome their backgrounds through strength of soul. It speaks for the superior powers of goodness that the reverse rarely happens; children who were loved seldom become cruel in adult life. We can count on it that harsh treatment of a young child will open channels to the forces of darkness but will not exclude the forces of light. Indeed, the light that radiates from such a soul can be of exceptional brilliance.

It should be realized that good and evil are not vague forces coming at us like a blowing fog but are energies transmitted by souls in spirit form. Nothing in the created worlds is formless. As we are embodied, so are the spirits who guide or retard our progress. They are spirits of light on the ascending path of universal service, or they are psychic entities of the downward stream. The division is far from clear cut—many spirits are seeking their direction; others are deluded or lost among the astral levels. We tune in to those levels according to our own. We open ourselves to their influence as we ourselves have been influenced in our growing years, but also through the use of our will. The will is the deciding factor. Once past the helplessness of childhood, we are the choosers of our fate. Other influences are those we have brought with us from our former lives, which all contribute to the formation of our will. Although we carry with us a degree of predetermination resulting from our choices in past lives, through our will we shall determine the direction of the present course.

Journey into Free Will

All of our lives have been preparation for soul comple-tion. Unconsciously we have followed the magnetic pull exerted by the lost twin and others of our soul family. As the destination nears, our efforts become in-creasingly conscious. At first we simply followed the will of God; now we are granted choice. We may choose to accord with God's will or oppose it. Thus we distinguish between good and evil. That ability is essential if we are not to be deflected as the goal comes in sight.

We have passed many tests in our long climb to the summit. But they do not become easier. Imagine that we are scaling a sunlit pyramid, with its far side in shadow. Above the apex is the pure light of consciousness, free of duality. In order for us to move into that light, we must meet the crucial test. For just at the tip, where we are closest to the light, we are also closest to the dark.

A great light attracts a great shadow. The potent stellar light generated by reunited twins cannot but be opposed by the counterforces. Once the twins have made connection and completed each other, they will be equipped to overcome future onslaughts and use them as steps in their growth. It is on the approach to the twin union that we are most at risk of being set back in our ascent.

Means of Protection

Many of us are afraid to admit the reality of evil. Yet safety lies in doing just that. We must recognize its existence in the world and in ourselves. Only then can we learn to identify and close off the avenues to the darker sides of our personalities. This requires a constant inner vigilance, and a vigilance also to the inroads of evil in the society around us.

Violence and brutal sexuality are now almost commonplace in our news reports, movies, television shows, and mass-market fiction. These derive their popularity from their appeal to the dark side in human nature. In looking at these images we hold up a mirror to ourselves. But the mirror is clouded, and we do not see. Horror movies, horror novels, enactments of hatred and cruelty, are poison to the soul. They infect us with toxic psychic substance, which after a time becomes part of our being. Every atom of it will have to be purged before we are ready to approach the sacred love of the soul, in the form of our twin.

We could avoid much of this contamination by boycotting popular "entertainment." As the twin-soul light begins to spread across the world, such a boycott will happen naturally. There will arise new entertainment forms that inspire rather than negate. These are already beginning to appear, with appeal to the audience that is ready, meaning the people who are ready for the twin.

The Duel of Light and Dark

Yet we need to understand that evil is serving its purpose, which is to advance the good. From the great heights of the spirit, the diabolical force is seen for what it is: a manifestation of cosmic darkness, which came into being with the first stirring of Creation. God willed that there be light, and light came forth from the void, and darkness with it. This was the fundamental duality of polar opposites, which existed thereafter on all planes below.

Then came the division of the Deity into its complementary opposites, masculine and feminine, and the subsequent reduction of these into the many. The purpose of the cosmic darkness was to aid the return of the myriad forms by providing opposition to them. At the universal level it holds the stars and planets in their orbits, preventing them from colliding. At the biological level it maintains the separations among molecules, resisting their attraction and creating solid substance. At the human stage it becomes personalized and demonized, shaped by the desires of individuals evolving into free will. It aids in the application of impersonal karmic law by providing the due share of suffering for the education of each human soul.

This is the goad that drives life upward. We may understand it better if we picture two duelists fighting their way up a broad staircase toward the heavens. One dualist, the Prince of Light, is above the other, the Prince of Darkness. Both are swift, nimble, and full of grace. They are evenly matched.

The Prince of Darkness perpetually jabs the Prince of Light and drives him farther up. Blood is drawn; it pours forth and scatters, its drops congealing into suns, adding brilliance to the scene. The duel is fight, but also play. The fighters play in dead earnest: worlds hang upon their every stroke. They do not tire, though they have been playing from time immemorial.

As they mount the staircase, all life mounts with them. The steps they have climbed stretch endlessly below. How high do they extend above? The summit is veiled in mist; we cannot see.

The same mist floats about the individual human mind as it struggles for clarity in its battle for ascendance. The demonic powers employ the weaknesses of the human being, but the human employs the demons as well. There is an exchange from below to above and above to below. The demonic powers, as long as they are able to operate in darkness, can proliferate. Living in the depths of the personality, they can store up and transmit their poison. But when they are released and brought to the light, they don't disappear; they join in a dance with the light powers and become alloyed with them. Raw instincts become sublimated and turned to service as the power for evil is transmuted into the power for good.

And look! The mist has cleared at the top of the cosmic staircase. The duel has become a dance. As part of the dance the two princes join hands. And now the uppermost prince lifts his brother, once Brother of the Shadow, and enthrones him in light by his side.

Recognizing the Twin

HOW MAY WE RECOGNIZE THE TWIN-SOUL RELA-
tionship? How is it distinct from any other good relationship? The difference is this: in a good relationship
two people proceed in harmony, reconciling their con-
flicting views; but the twin-soul relationship is founded
on a fundamental sense of oneness: oneness of vision,
oneness of purpose, oneness of feeling. Twin souls do
not pull in separate ways, except briefly and temporarily at the personality level. They progress as one, no
longer hobbled by differences in pace or direction. This
is the reason their advance is so swift once the connection has been made.

Twin souls have a oneness of vision. Everyone
stands at a different place on the mountain of evolution. No two views are alike, yet each is true for the
viewer. The scene is radically different from opposite
sides of the mountain, only slightly different for those
whose course has brought them near to each other.
None but twin souls stand exactly in the same place.

They see with one eye, the third eye, the instrument of spiritual vision. This is not to deny the individuality in their personal way of looking at that same vista. But the differences between them complement and enhance each other's perceptions. If this were not so, then the singleness of their vision would fail to engage and excite each other's interest. The balance of creative tension between them is their promise of increase and final perfection as cocreators.

Twin souls do not doubt that they have been brought together for a reason. That reason may unfold gradually, but it *will* unfold as a result of their focused attention, for they are aware in their depths that life is nothing if not the fulfillment of divine purpose. In their preparation for each other, they have been finely tuning their sense of where they want to go. Therefore they will dedicate themselves, as one, to the chosen service for which they are destined.

Twin souls have a oneness of feeling. It is in their love that the oneness of twin souls is most recognizable, but this is far beyond romantic love. It is soul love, extending beyond the individuals to the whole. The injunction to love one's neighbor as oneself is an ideal difficult to truly obey, for we cannot feel as our neighbor feels. There is still separation. With twin souls there is no separation (individual selfhood, yes, but no longer division). Only the twin can be loved as himself or herself, in oneness of feeling, for each half is the self of the other.

There is no competition between twin souls. One-upmanship is unheard of; neither would wish to be above the other, nor to diminish the other. Twin-soul love is recognized by its harmlessness; there is no deliberate wounding, no missiles aimed at each other, never a punitive impulse. If there is hurt through omission or error, each feels the other's hurt almost before it is inflicted. Exquisite care is exercised to exclude any pain but growing pain.

We want to emphasize that the twin-soul reality is also an ideal. It is a pattern for all relationships and attainable to a large degree by women and men of goodwill on the way to full soul realization.

The First Encounter

The first meeting between twin souls is likely to have a memorable quality. On the spiritual level it is a momentous event, and the significance reverberates into this life. Events then tend to move swiftly, as though locking two souls into place, like the two spirit rings, which have always been interlocked in the heights.

In one instance a woman was introduced at a party to a well-known speaker, a scientist whose work she had long admired. She congratulated him and told him of her respect. He looked at her, almost hypnotically, and found himself suddenly moved to say, "We will be working together in the future." He was surprised, for he was not a man given to prophecy or any kind of psychic phenomena. It was as if the words had simply passed through his lips. She felt an energy emanating from him and was stirred with a strange excitement that would lead before long to the recognition that they were twin souls. They did in fact join their lives in a common work, contributing to new scientific knowledge. They never forgot the drama of their meeting.

Drama may well attend the twin-soul encounter, for the theme itself is the essence of drama. A particularly memorable experience is rendered in Ingaret Giffard's autobiography, *The Way Things Happen.* The wife of the distinguished author Laurens van der Post, she writes of their first meeting, on a ship bound for South Africa, his homeland: "When we talked it was not as if we had only just met, but as though we had never been parted."

One afternoon they went down to his cabin and simply lay on his bunk with their arms around each other. Of this she writes:

> It had not been an erotic indulgence; it had not been an expression of physical attraction. It was a human experience; but it was also something beyond human understanding. As I lay there in

Laurens' arms I felt that somehow we had both
put our personal signature at the bottom of one
of the more closely-written pages of life itself.
When at last we rose I knew that, although I was
the same person, there was one profound difference. I was no longer alone; in fact I could never be
alone again. Things would go wrong, of course, but
when they did, and I could totally share the experience with another human being, that would change
the texture of the calamity, because it could be contained in the *rightness* of our consummated communion. These were poor words, I knew, with which to
express the feeling of life's inevitability, brought
into being by our common self-recognition. . . . It
was a state of being and of belonging that was not
in the world of ordinary affairs.

This is pure soul recognition, breaking through all
mental barriers, surpassing the downward pull of intellectual reasoning. It is the reconnecting of two individuals formed from the substance of one soul, breathing
a common air, carrying in their deepest parts the memory of their undivided state. These and other com-
monalities will be found in all twin souls.

Commonalities and Differences

Twins will be the same in aspiration, intensity of being,
capacity for love, dedication to others and to the highest

in themselves. They will have in common a faith in life, in the goodness behind all things; for if they did not believe in the supremacy of goodness, they would not be ready for the great good of each other. They will be alike in sensitivity, in appreciation of beauty, and in acceptance of its opposite. They will exhibit to the same degree persistence as well as strength of will and fortitude in adversity.

By their samenesses we will know them. As on the veins of a leaf, the same pattern of energies will reproduce itself throughout the whole life of the twins. Their counterbalance is most clearly indicated in the choice of lifework. Our experiences have shown that twin souls, more often than not, will be engaged in complementary aspects of the same work.

Both may be healers, in different areas of the healing profession, or both musicians, one a performer and one a composer, supporting and completing the other. Both may deal with language, the one using spoken words, the other written. In such a case the speaker would have a gift for writing, and the writer for speaking. Beyond the words, both would be driven by a similar compelling interest.

As the lives of the twins interconnect, their experiences converge, leading to combined work of higher fulfillment.

They might both be active in the new enlightening

thought that is appearing in the churches. They might be agents and impresarios, furthering the work of artists and innovators; perhaps they are publishers, alive to the responsibility of bringing the new spiritual literature to the public. They might be teachers, social workers, or businesspersons, espousing ethics and responsibility in the business world. In whatever field, they are sure to be performing a work of service.

In general, people can be grouped into two categories of intellectual preference, one with a scientific mental set and the other an artistic mental set. The examples of twin souls that we know indicate that twins are of the same mental cast. Observing married couples, we note that a mix of artistic and scientific temperaments does not conduce to the same harmony as that between two artistic types or two scientists.

Of course there are all gradations in between. While some twins have a harmony of like mind, in others the complementary qualities may be stronger and their love thrives on the difference. The evidence of their twinship is the harmony of sustained love.

If the twins' work is not in the same general area, they will share the same vision. They may approach the ideal from opposite sides. Fundamentally the same, they constantly broaden each other's scope through the play of their complementary energies. Since they have a common origin, twins have a commonality of likes, dislikes, tastes, and aesthetic preferences. Usually they favor the same type of music. They have a matching sense of humor, and may have similar social skills, manifesting in complementary ways. They have many of the same tastes in food, in recreational activities, in entertainment. Both may like cold weather or hot; both may love the sea or the mountains. For some, these combine in a general love of nature. Other twins perhaps prefer city life.

Their handwriting may show similarities, for graphology is a great revealer of character. The life map of the palm is etched similarly in each, possibly with a matching line of Mars, of intuition, of mental power. If one is sweet-natured, so is the other. It is, in fact, axiomatic that twin souls are good-natured, for the higher the spiritual evolution, the more joyful is the spirit.

They are twins, and their twinship runs throughout their life, in thoughts and physical makeup. The twin souls' underlying similarities find a parallel in the case of identical twins who are separated in infancy and adopted by different parents. If they meet as adults, they often find that they tend to dress the same way, cut their hair the same way, are engaged in the same kind of work, and show other similar inclinations, even to the extent of having married the same kind of person.

In balanced proportion to twin-soul samenesses are the differences. These provide the necessary creative tension, the momentum for action, and the fuel to lift the combined unit upward.

The primacy of intellect or emotion may differ between the twins. The two must engage on the field of friendly battle and, through the stimulation of struggle, arrive at harmonious expression of their individual selves. Clouds may at times gather over the scene. Dark forces, ever on the alert, will seize any opportunity to create misunderstanding. The twins must test their spiritual muscle against each other, constantly confirming their equality of strength, perpetually adding to the strength. The sun disappears and is forgotten in the moment of crisis. When the sun emerges, there is a rush of joy as it uplifts the souls with renewed spiritual force.

The Gift of Twinship

According to the Sufi text, twinship is a gift. The gift may be accepted hesitantly at first. Realization of twinship is a process, a path of discovery, opening steadily and widening into recognition. The twin may be encountered on several occasions before true conscious recognition happens. These occasions prepare the personality to deal with the intensity of the connection, as well as with the life circumstances that the twin brings to the relationship.

The recognition may even begin on subtle levels before the meeting itself occurs. As the twins draw near, they are likely to become increasingly aware that the right person could be anywhere about. They begin to trust their inner sensing more and more, remaining alert to the situation, ready to recognize the opportunity of a lifetime when it does appear.

Circumstances create opportunities for bringing the twins together when the moment is right. Soul recognition is an extremely powerful moment, the occasion when the spark leaps from one to the other, the flame is lit, and the divided soul instantaneously becomes one.

Paradoxically, though completion occurs in an instant it is also a process of growth. Time is necessary for the new consciousness to take hold and work its way through the complex personalities that enclose the soul. And the completing is a continuous activity that has been a long time gathering and will strengthen throughout life.

The trustworthy signal of the twin recognition and the arrival of the gift is an immediate sense of unconditional love, a love that becomes increasingly conscious once the recognition is openly accepted. This is perhaps the most profound experience of meeting and recognizing the twin.

We might wonder how love can be unconditional

when there has been no time for it to develop. But there has been time, all the time in the world: the time of the soul's evolution up to this point. The twins do not regard each other in the same manner as others might: they never see each other as flawed persons but always as pure souls. They "cognize" the true being of the other. That light of purity dominates the vision, not blinding them to the flaws in each other but lifting them above the duality of approval and disapproval, illumining the whole, making all of it beloved.

All twin-soul meetings have important features in common, though the descriptions are unique and varied.

One person talks about twin-soul recognition in this way:

> It could be described as the difference between watching a small portable television in black and white and going to a brand-new state-of-the-art cinema and seeing the whole thing in full color with surround sound.

Another fulfilled twin shares this picture:

> You are both on a roller coaster of intensity as the experience of being together almost literally sweeps you off your feet. The only way to describe the experience is like being lifted for a while to a state of consciousness that is beyond space and

time, and from which you will never be the same
again. The feeling is one of an end to loneliness
for the first time in life and of having found someone who understands you deeply without the need
for complicated explanations. You feel as if you
have always known this person—it is like a home-
coming, although on the level of the personality
there may be some catching up to do. There is a
feeling of a great sense of purpose and meaning to
the relationship, as if there is an opportunity to be
of real service in some way. There is also a huge
sense of relief after the long experience of preparation and search, and above all, an awareness that
the journey has really only just begun!

Mutual Recognition

Will recognition of twinship always be mutual? At
soul level it cannot be otherwise. The twin sparks from
the soul immediately fly together when the two persons
make connection. Yet there may sometimes be resistance, for emotional or practical reasons.

A man in a distinguished position, married, and
with a family could understandably be thrown into
turmoil when suddenly confronted with the other half
of his soul. In such a case there may be refusal to acknowledge the twinship. Yet souls come together at the
choosing of destiny. They meet at the exact point in

their evolution when the polarities *must* unite. The soul does not wait for the road ahead to be perfectly smooth and clear. The universal forces will bring all elements into alignment in the course of the struggle. Finally the magnetic attraction between the twins will be so powerful that all obstacles will be overcome. Solutions will be found. No challenge is given to the soul without a solution hidden somewhere within.

Then there are instances of delusion in which twinship is falsely proclaimed.

Forcing the Fit

In our desire for completion we are at risk of seeing the twin where the twin is not, caught up in the glamour of the ideal of true spiritual union. There is a human tendency to try to shape a relationship into what we wish it to be. We seize upon certain similarities between ourselves and our partners, magnifying them out of proportion while blinding ourselves to important differences that must be addressed in the end. We can easily slip into a fantasy realm where we create the illusion of the twin, in a denial of predestination.

All is not predestined; our present destiny, formed through the karma of past choices, still allows us some choice. Our twin soul, however, has been destined from the beginning of creation. It is not a matter of choice;

either the person is a twin or isn't. No amount of wishing or manipulating can make it otherwise.

Consider our fingerprints. Where can we find an identical set? Can we take another at random and re-carve the designs on the ends of the fingers? We are attempting as much when we try to remodel another person into our image of the twin. True twins do not try to change each other.

What begins as mild self-deception can lead us into the deep waters of delusion. In that treacherous sea the soul can be carried far from the twin, perhaps for a lifetime, still holding the belief that the one-and-only other half has appeared. Astral forces of delusion are ever ready to delay the soul on the pretext of advancement. Under this influence a false radiance dazzles the eye and distorts the vision. Such a force is described in spiritual literature as the Luciferan light, the light that blinds. To those in its grip this light cannot be distinguished from true spiritual illumination. Religious fanatics, cultists, and false prophets have fallen prey to this delusionary light.

For our purpose, one illustration will suffice: A mother of five fell under the magnetic influence of a charismatic spiritual leader who had encountered the theory of twinship during his studies and convinced her that they were twin souls. She was persuaded to leave her family and to live with him in his colony. Not long afterward, he was attracted to another woman among his followers. He proclaimed that she, too, was his twin soul and that in rare instances the soul was divided into three, not two.

In all relations between people, the soul is reaching for its group and its twin. But our ego reach is of a different order from that of the soul. Lacking truth, it cannot convey that inner feeling of conviction, satisfaction, and sublimity that signals the true fit. Martin Israel, a British parish priest, author, and minister of healing who has traveled widely conducting retreats, gives us these words of wisdom: "I feel that when people seek the Kingdom of God with their full being, much more will be added as well, including an encounter with their twin soul. Too much search for a twin soul could have selfish overtones, and divert one from doing one's work properly in the immediate future."

Only when the twin-soul encounter is God-guided will there be a true and genuine fit. Otherwise the forcing of the fit continues in its many forms. One of these is the idealization of the love partner, an idealization that can be carried to extremes and is caused by our harboring deep in the soul the image of the ideal complement. Driven by loneliness we may seize upon the ready partner and force the belief that our ideal has been met. In order to validate the belief, we repress our own needs. The falsity is rationalized away. Others can see the mis-fitting where we cannot.

One needn't be a psychoanalyst to see through such illusions; but a trained observer may see through them to specific causes. Coauthor Maurie Pressman tells of a woman being treated by him for depression. She had been married for many years and had borne three children. All this time her husband had been extremely critical and had cruelly carped at her. The woman reported these incidents but showed no anger or affect. The analyst heard instead an idealization of the man and a repeated affirmation that he was always right. It became clear that the patient was agreeing with her husband's criticisms so that she could repress her hostility toward him. By making him perfect, she had no cause for anger and could continue in the illusion that she was happily married. In so doing she was delaying her progress in life, and his as well—and also that of her twin soul, who is affected in absentia.

Whether we pursue our completion by the short route or the long, we are driven by the same need, to reach the light of consciousness and joy. This is the purpose of our existence and the purpose for which so many twin souls are drawing together on the earth at this time.

Realizing the Purpose

It is believed by many that humanity is on the brink of a quantum leap in consciousness. Enlightened people are preparing themselves for this in their own ways, realizing it is time for us to awaken to our origins and our potential and take responsibility for ourselves and for the earth.

We believe that twin souls have a special contribution to make; their coming together in numbers at this time has a reason at both the individual and planetary level.

When twin souls join, they generate a vortex of energy that may be seen as a light in the darkness of society's unconsciousness. In completing each other, the whole becomes greater than the sum of its parts: the two create three, and the third is a very potent force, a force of light and love at an extremely pure level. This kind of energy, which partakes of the energy of both twins, is different from that of individuals or even groups of people working together. It is the special offering that the twins have to give to each other and expend in service to humanity.

The image we see is of a dark auditorium lit by an increasing number of individual flames. Each flame represents the conscious and harmonious relationship between twin souls. Eventually, as the twins multiply, there will be so many flames, so much light, and so much energy of that particular sort on the planet that it will act as a catalyst and help to bring about the expected breakthrough of consciousness.

This helps us to see that the search for the twin is not selfishness but service. The drawing together of twin souls is the first and best hope of the world. And how will their lives conjoin? The matter is perfectly simple for those who direct the traffic of the universe. It was all set in motion with the first breath of God, and each moving part involving every other throughout the infinitude of cosmic dimensions is keyed to receive the signal when it comes; and oceans will part and mountains will move and the affairs of nations will fall still to make way for two hands outstretched at the moment of their time.

Sex: Union of Body and Soul

FOLLOWING THE ACT OF CREATION, THE DIVISION of the One into the many, there arose a potent force that would rule throughout the vastness of the whole, restoring it to oneness. This force is the irresistible compulsion to union, activating every created form, from single atoms to solar systems. In human beings the force is manifest as the sexual drive.

Human sexual desire is a response to the call of the soul to unite with another soul through the instrument of the body. The impulse travels through the many levels of spirit and mind, recognizable by the senses as a drive toward pleasure. If controlled by the shadow side of the individual, the pleasure drive may be perverted and act as a separating rather than unifying force. The source is the same. The soul, close to the divine origin of bliss, seeks the joy that it knows is the nature of union.

Sexual urgency in the lower animals is a blind instinct. Angelic beings, also experiencing the law of attraction, will be fully awakened to sexual magnetism in its ascended form. It is for the human in the middle realm, part animal, part angel, to combine passion and transcendent bliss in the ritual of love.

Sexual pleasures increase throughout the rising planes of being. They can be made to increase here and now in the vessel of the body, with its attendant spiritual bodies, lifting us to communion with our soul. The magnetic power that we know as sex is a bridge connecting all the levels of existence.

The tie between body and soul appears in an energy sequence that is repeated throughout nature. In human sexuality it assumes the pattern of tension, release, ecstasy, and relaxation. The act of sexual union creates a buildup of energy to a near-intolerable level, its urgencies filling every cell of the body until they break the bonds of the body in an eruption into cosmic bliss. Orgasm induces a propulsion of the self into the All. In this state of bliss and lost consciousness of the self, one is in the rapture of joining, in timelessness, space-lessness, the void that is nevertheless full.

It was Wilhelm Reich who drew attention to the basic design that governs the flow of the life force. Reich, a disciple of Freud, revealed that emotional resistances were reflected in the body. The life force was impeded by these blocks. He saw that the basic formula for the stream of life, from the amoeba to the great blue whale to man and woman themselves, was reflected in the sexual lifestream. The free flow of that force he considered a necessity for health and well-being.

Reich studied the flow of libido, or love energy, in terms of the impediments that obstruct its course. His treatment for his patients was directed toward releasing interference to enable them to become expressive personalities with full freedom of sexual expression. Where sexual energy was constricted by emotional blocks, he endeavored to remove the blocks so that the flow could lead to full orgastic release. He saw in this pattern a picture of the life flow itself. In life everywhere on the planet, the pattern is repeated of accumulated charge, release, relaxed equilibrium.

Reich's pioneering work was elaborated by his followers John and Eva Pierrakos, who pointed out how the physical body and spiritual bodies intermesh in the pleasurable experience of full flow. Their thinking is consistent with Eastern teachings about our descent from the highest vibrations into energy bodies ("subtle bodies"), which are transmitted, in step-down fashion, through the etheric net that surrounds the physical body. It is this etheric net that contains the universal energy called *prana* in India, *chi* in China, and named *orgone* by Wilhelm Reich. These higher bodies surround and influence the physical body during our life on earth.

We quote from a lecture on *The Full Pulsation of Life*, given by Eva Pierrakos.

> A very liberated human being with few or no blocks or inhibitions, without distortion or negativity, is capable of a high degree of pleasure, for then the energy of the subtle bodies penetrates the surface body. Only then, when a high degree of bliss is experienced, will the person deeply know that human pleasure is essentially the same as the cosmic state of bliss, that they are not opposites, but one and the same. Real pleasure is intensely fleshly and intensely spiritual. There is no division between the fleshly and spiritual state. The ultimate state of liberation, of cosmic being, is total pleasure. *The ultimate reality is pleasure.*
>
> Bliss is the natural state of a unified being in harmony with himself and the universe. By this we mean a state of physical and spiritual bliss that is experienced in every particle of one's body and soul, of the outer and inner being, with all sensations and faculties alive, awake and feeling. This state is very much a present reality. It is your birthright, my friends. Your longing for it is the most real and healthy movement within yourself.
>
> Pleasure is a state in which your entire being vibrates and pulsates undividedly, in harmony with itself and the universe, and hence with an-

other human being. There is no division within
you, no doubt about the rightfulness of your bliss.
You feel no guilt or hesitation. On the contrary,
you will deeply feel that the greater your ecstasy,
your pleasure, and your joy, the more you contribute to the world.

When we reach this inner awareness, we will make
the total experience of pleasure a spiritual and practical goal. We will work to remove all inner obstructions to the flow of the life force within us. In order
to live intimately and completely with our bodies,
our souls, and our spirits, there must be a full growth
and ripening of the personality. This occurs when
we have become able to carry on a fulfilled sexual
relationship.

Such a relationship means that we have overcome
the fears and restrictions that have been put upon us in
the past. We have rid ourselves of shame and guilt
about sex. We recognize that sexual pleasure is a true
gift of heaven. We have grown beyond sexual and personal selfishness. We have respect for ourselves, for the
wisdom of the body and our own needs as well as for
the needs of the other, so that we can listen to them
and satisfy them, fulfill them, rejoice in them in a way
that brings us and the other into a glowing joie de vivre.

A full blossoming of love makes us want to fulfill

and complete the love partner. We desire to give sexual pleasure and be stimulated by it while showing tenderness and concern and being fulfilled by the joy of the beloved.

The full sexual relationship is a sacred communion between one human being and another, leading to a soul relationship and preparing the way for communion with the twin, whether in this lifetime or the next. It means that the two are capable of a lasting sexual and personal bond. The full sexual relationship therefore tends to be built on a lasting relationship and builds a lasting relationship in turn. It helps to protect against the dulling of sexual desire, which can occur as a consequence of a long-standing marriage. Constant fulfillment builds an upstream, a welling up of both love and desire.

Each can surrender to the needs of the body, allowing a full flow of genital release and full joining on all levels of being. Such a relationship releases the body from its urgent needs; it releases the stores of love so that they can flow and surround the love partners. Such a release allows us to apply our energy to other social fulfillments and to make social contributions rather than to pursue temporary satisfactions in a vain attempt to heal our fragmentation.

The Spiritual Partnership

The union of sex and love shows the way to union with the Divine. This fact has been recognized in the highest realms of spiritual wisdom, if not by most organized religions. Jewish mysticism teaches certain techniques for raising sexual energy to celestial realms. The very first written description of Jewish meditation is found in a marriage manual, *The Holy Letter*, attributed to the kabalist Joseph Gikatille.

And as described in Tabi Aryeh Kaplan's *Jewish Meditation*, the partners meditate throughout the sexual act, becoming "aware of the spark of the Divine in the pleasure itself and elevating it to its source." According to a contemporary Hasidic description by Yitzhak Buxbaum in *Jewish Spiritual Practices*, "The *Zohar* teaches that when man and woman in sex are both directed to Divine presence, the Divine Presence rests on their bed.... (It is taught that) a man should make his house a Temple and his bedroom a Holy of Holies."

In Jewish mystical thought, then, there is a sacralization of the erotic and an eroticization of the sacred.

The idea needs no explanation to twin souls like Giselle and Andrew. Here Giselle takes us into their Holy of Holies, the bedroom:

> We always meditate before lovemaking. So,
> when we make love it is not out of lack, but out

of fullness—a fullness of love, and of feeling loved by God. It is a real connection. And so we are not there to be fulfilled but to fulfill the other. I go into my sexual self with a desire to explore. I don't go into it as a way of being loved, because I *am* love. I know it. And because of that I attain states of ecstasy that are much more fulfilling than if I were to depend on a man to create my experience. I am more than a participant, I am a creator. I am more than satisfied, because my ecstasy is creating a space where nothing else is needed.

It's not a sexual *part* that I want to fulfill; my *whole body* is a sexual thing. Because of that, my exploration of it really brings me into the light-energy of creation. It's a blend of loving my husband and a search for the light that my whole self is going for, when we make love. This is the ultimate love experience. I'm not looking for a local experience, i.e., vaginal orgasm or clitoral orgasm. No, I want the highest, the most that I can get.

I don't go for regular physical orgasms because I don't need to. I'm more satisfied without that. I stop and am happy. Not that I restrain my sexual energy; I channel it so that my whole body is illumined by it, not just a small part of myself. Andrew too—he joins me more and more in that way—although at times he needs the physical climax.

The way I see it, unless you let the other person explore his sexuality through you (not including violence, of course, never violence) there is no need of being a couple. If one can't offer himself or herself to the other, what is the need of the relationship? With the kind of sexuality I practice, I find it quite easy to be always available to my husband. I am energized by my sexuality, because we make love to create more love, more energy to serve the world. By our happiness and joy, we can create more, give more.

Our sexuality creates a space where we can step back from all the things that have happened in the day; the body can step away and calm down and connect itself to the source of life, the creative energy inside. I can't tell you how much happier I am now that I experience sex life that way with Andrew.

When I go to bed with Andrew I look at him as a divine being. I see him as being God, and I am bathing in his love. He knows that I love him to the utmost of his capacity, the most of what he can be. As I go to him my desire is to connect with him as his most beautiful self. When I feel my skin beside his skin, there is a radiance created, because we have nothing, *nothing* in between us that is negative.

I believe that inside of everybody there is the intention of being perfect and truly loving—and that's the part of him that I want to connect with when we go to bed. Behind our sexuality there is a door to the unlimited self that we are, the divine light behind the curtain of our body. By truly loving each other we go through that door and there is no need to search for more pleasure.

Giselle and Andrew are part of the shift from traditional marriage to spiritual partnerships that have more conscious states of being and ways of relating. Marriage was originally designed to assist physical survival. With the growth of spiritual consciousness in the world, that model is being replaced by another: a sacred commitment between partners to assist each other's spiritual growth.

Gary Zukav writes about spiritual partnership in *Seat of the Soul,* saying that spiritual partners know clearly that the reason they are together has to do with the evolution of their souls. Because spiritual partners can see from this perspective, they engage in a very different dynamic than do husbands and wives. The conscious evolution of the soul is not part of the structural dynamic of marriage.

Spiritual, or sacred, partners understand that they are together in a committed relationship, but that commitment is not to physical security. It is rather to each other's spiritual growth, recognizing that spiritual growth is their purpose on earth and everything else must serve that. The duration of their partnership is determined by how long it is appropriate for their evolution to be together. All the vows that a human being can make cannot prevent the spiritual path from exploding through and breaking those vows if the spirit must move on. It is appropriate for spiritual partners to remain together only as long as they grow together. Just as external power is no longer appropriate to our evolution, the archetype of marriage is no longer appropriate.

This does not mean that the institution of marriage will disappear overnight. Marriages will continue to exist, but marriages that succeed will only succeed with the consciousness of spiritual partnership.

In the following twin history we see how sexual union can occur even when the partners are not physically together.

Transmutation to Higher Realms of Love

Alexandra was not entirely happy in her marriage. There was a lack of fulfillment, which she did not completely recognize until Leroy came into her life. Leroy and she are both musicians. He is a virtuoso violinist, whose concerts keep him on tour most of the year. Alexandra is a pianist by training and teaches the instrument to her three children and other students.

She and Leroy were drawn together when she attended one of his concerts. After the performance she felt an irresistible inner command to go backstage and meet him. The moment they shook hands they were subject to the mysterious pull of the soul, the ancient link reaffirming itself.

Twin-soul love grew rapidly, but the circumstances were not conducive to its full consummation. Alexandra had loyalties to her family, which her conscience would not allow her to abandon. Leroy was unattached but wedded to his work, locked into his extended concert schedule.

Despite his busy schedule, he began phoning her from his concert stops. Through long phone conversations and the correspondence that developed, their compatibilities were revealed, and their bond strengthened. Limited as they were by their outer circumstances, they reached inwardly toward each other with growing fervor.

Nothing stands still, certainly not love that is released from long confinement. There is an expansion of being that accompanies soul-love, and no force on earth can restrict it. Both Alexandra and Leroy are mystical and spiritually aware people, yet well grounded in the practical realities of their lives. But spiritual forces were at work beyond the constraints of earthly life.

The meeting of souls is serious business to those who oversee the intertwining fates in the great patterns of return. A soul union, which is destined, will fulfill itself in the best possible way for all whose lives are touched by it as long as those involved remain open to their center of truth, their intuition, the channel to the highest good.

By whatever means, the soul *will* have its way. If intolerable restrictions are present, it will break through with supersensory powers for those in whom it dwells, always provided that they are ready for such powers. The force of the soul is the same as that which drives the great cataracts of nature. It cannot be stopped by any law but its own.

The first intimations of powers beyond the ordinary that Alexandra experienced was her response to Leroy's voice. After speaking with him on the phone, she would find herself suffused with radiant energy, an energy previously felt only in the exaltation of great music or in rare heights of meditation. The energy built as the bond between them grew. After they had talked, Alexandra found that she lay awake the entire night in a mysterious joy and elevation of mind, passing into timelessness so that the night seemed all too short.

The infusion of energy was so great that it remained

throughout the following day. She had discovered something more restorative than sleep. It was love energy, the energy of the cosmos. It was sex energy, reunited with its birth stream, love: love and sex transcendent.

Each telephone conversation produced one of these peak experiences. For two or three nights in a row Alexandra could forgo sleep. She described the sensation:

> I felt an expansion of myself into a huge force field composed of light and swirling color. The feeling was of vibrant activity, like a dance of atoms that I could plainly *see*, for I felt as though I had become transparent. It was bliss, I was made of bliss, and I understood that every atom of everything is made of bliss. At times I was transported into a great stillness, when all the atoms came to a perfect standstill. The bliss was even greater in the stillness. I stopped breathing so as not to shatter it, and remembered the words: *Be still and know that I am God.*

There is little doubt that Alexandra was experiencing a spontaneous opening of the chakra centers and a flow of kundalini. This is the universal power transmitted to and through the human being and described as the serpent power coiled at the base of the spine. On being aroused, it flows through all the energy centers to the brain, bringing with it a tremendous energy, sometimes resulting in enlightenment.

Normally the kundalini and chakra energies are stimulated into activity through specific yoga disciplines. Alexandra had engaged in none of these, except meditation. Her experience revealed that the energy system can spring open under the stimulus of spiritual practice and love.

Then Alexandra found that clairvoyant faculties, which she had never experienced before, were unfolding swiftly. Awakening suddenly one night, she had a startling vision. She described it to Leroy in a letter:

> It was a vision, but it was a happening, too. I
> was in it and observing it all at once. I saw you in
> a spiritual realm. I was there standing near you,
> watching as a river of golden light poured into
> you through the top of your head. It poured and
> poured. I was astonished at your capacity for this
> light. It seemed it would never stop. But then it
> did. You looked at me and took a step toward me.
> I stepped toward you. Then we simply flowed into
> each other. You entered me, I entered you, wholly
> and in every part. We became one body, and with
> this came a rapture that struck through me like
> a shaft of lightning. I felt it physically and with

new spiritual senses that seemed suddenly to have sprung open.

This visionary experience proved to be an initiation into astral travel. Not long afterward, as Alexandra was getting into bed—she and her husband sleep in separate rooms—she suddenly saw Leroy standing there at the foot. The sight scarcely surprised her; it seemed completely natural. She said inwardly and calmly, Oh, there's Leroy, as though he had just entered her room in person. She attributed the naturalness to the knowledge that they were one in spirit. In the spiritual dimension there is no space, and so he was easily present in astral form. At the same time she felt a breeze passing over her face and hands and experienced an unusual sensation in the throat.

In her experience they made love. Alexandra described the lovemaking as being verbal and telepathic, as their astral bodies duplicated physical movements with great passion and exchange of love. Penetration was not localized, rather a complete fusion of their spirit bodies took place. The effect for Alexandra was an exquisite thrilling throughout her whole body, including the sexual zones, coupled with high spiritual joy and pleasure.

The event moved into timelessness—which later

proved to be two hours by the clock—and continued with intensity and exaltation, yet mixed with spreading peacefulness and calm. The great discovery was that peace, rather than excitement, brought forth the purest bliss.

In place of physical orgasm, the bliss took wing; Alexandra experienced a tremendous lifting effect, a soaring, as though, she said, together she and Leroy were jetting into the cosmos "like a shooting star silently exploding, sending down a shower of sparks which washed around us in spirals of indescribable, soft sensation, swelling my heart and mind." There followed an absolute stillness, the contemplative stillness described by mystics.

This is sacred sexuality, the transcendent spiritual sex, which does not deny the body but more fully engages it, opening from it greater founts of ecstasy. Here we have an example of the higher plane melting into the material.

The experience took place within Alexandra's consciousness and no doubt in Leroy's higher consciousness. It entered his brain-memory only at one point: Alexandra had felt her attention drawn to the clock and had noted the hour, eleven, just before seeing Leroy in her room. The next evening, talking with him on the telephone, separated again by earthly miles, she told him what had happened and wondered if he remembered. He did not, but asked, "What time was that?" Then he added quickly, "Don't tell me! Wait a minute . . . eleven o'clock! At eleven o'clock—it was nine o'clock here— I thought about visiting you."

"That's exactly when you appeared," said Alexandra with a sense of wonder.

Their separation had forced their souls to break through the boundaries of time and space. Once broken, the boundaries could not contain them again. An ascension was taking place within them both, in accordance with the purpose of twin-soul love, which is advancement, upliftment, the transmutation of the lower to the higher. They were learning to use their subtle bodies to acquaint themselves with the temples of the spiritual life, wherein ecstasy is the rule, not the exception.

The first of our finer vehicles is the etheric body, which duplicates and interpenetrates the physical body and does not leave it until the moment of death. Next is the astral body, which is free to travel and, in fact, departs during sleep. Highly evolved people, such as the spiritual masters, can send their astral forms abroad on specific missions while in waking consciousness they remain occupied with everyday earthly activities. Beyond the astral body is the finer mental body. Although our soul in its full dimension dwells simultaneously on every plane, the three lower worlds of the physical, astral, and mental are all we can grasp at the human stage.

It seems evident from Alexandra and Leroy's experiences that one or more of the bodies beyond the astral come into play in their spiritual lovemaking. Physical indications may be present as well. Alexandra received two unmistakable physical, sensory signals of Leroy's presence. One was a gentle activation of the throat, explainable as follows: eventually the energies of the lower chakras in the body must be transmuted and lifted up to the higher. A vital step is the raising of the sacral (reproductive) energy to the throat chakra, signifying the transmutation of the process of physical procreation to that of creative expression. In Alexandra the activating of the throat chakra was a spiritual-sexual response to the presence of the twin soul.

Her second sensory sign was the "breeze." In *The Secret Doctrine,* H. P. Blavatsky informs us that a spirit visiting a sensitive person will be felt as a passing breeze.

No words, Alexandra says, can express the beauty and the bliss of these encounters. Nevertheless, she continually attempted to describe them in her letters to Leroy as the visits occurred for the most part when he was asleep and vacating his physical body. He had no clear recollection of them, as we have little or no recollection of our visits to the spirit plane in sleep.

Yet we are given flashes of memory, and Leroy, too, had intimations and reverberations that reached his consciousness.

On one occasion he awoke suddenly in the night to sense himself soaring through cosmic spaces, joined with Alexandra. When he spoke to her the following evening he found that she had been experiencing a "visitation" at the same hour. On other occasions he saw her floating above his bed as a Chagall angel and felt a slight breeze on his lips.

Here Alexandra describes for Leroy one of their spiritual love meetings:

> Sometimes you lift my spirit right out of me; I feel you lifting it, so tenderly, like a mother gently raising a child up from its cradle. As this happens I become keenly aware of your spirit body, its racing vibrations, its brilliant colors. Then all of these stream into me, passing through and through and through me in waves of rapture. We engage in hours of pure ecstasy, no longer two lovers acting upon one another but one bliss weaving back and forth within itself. I will never get used to the passage of time when this happens, two hours or more as a rule. When I finally glance at the clock I can't believe what it is telling me, for I have been in timelessness, in eternity.

This is the true experience of heaven. You have brought me to it. How can I speak my adoration? It's the adoration of God, God in thee, and of the sure promise that it will be like this for everyone.

Let me describe it more from this earthly perspective. This is not just an ecstasy of mind! This is thoroughly physical, a sensation as of pure golden sunlight spreading open all the fibers of the body and filling them up with pleasure— something beyond pleasure, the very source of pleasure. It is subtly, excruciatingly orgastic, as if the entire physical structure trembles on the very edge of that precipice. This is because it is being experienced in the body as well as engaging all the other finer vehicles. It is total. It wants nothing but to remain, to be, to continue, it is sufficient to itself. It is perfect peace and being-ness.

But now Alexandra faced a marriage dilemma. Her husband, Vernon, had not failed to notice her happiness, while over the past months their sexual life had ceased. She was not prepared to leave her children to go traveling with Leroy, and this was not necessary to their soul completion in any case. They accepted that it was not their destiny to share a life of physical closeness.

She felt compelled, finally, to tell Vernon the truth

of what had been happening, and he was greatly shocked. He tried desperately to reclaim her. They both suffered the pains of growth in the necessary shift to a new way of being together. This was the challenge that Vernon's lifepath had placed before him. He was not to lure his wife back into the old marriage pattern but was to allow himself to be led by the spirit into the new. Without knowing it, this would inevitably set him on the course toward his own twin.

Eventually he learned to accept Alexandra's soul relationship with another. They forged a new friendship, still living in the same house, sharing the care of their children and liberating each other to fulfill their needs: Vernon's to find another physical partner, and Alexandra's to continue bonding with her twin. In time, under his wife's influence, Vernon found his way onto his own spiritual path.

As the years passed, Alexandra and Leroy grew in closeness, despite geographical separation. In this, they demonstrate two things: the soul knows no distance and the union of twin souls is an ongoing process.

Leroy had remarked to her, "We're like two mirrors reflecting each other." The mirror image carried across the world as easily as in the same room. He had also observed, "I am becoming more like you, and more like myself." It is a fascinating paradox that as twin souls wed their spirits ever more closely, then ever more strongly their individual natures emerge. In becoming more alike, they adopt each other's strengths and apply these in turn to their own self-unfolding—thus continually opening new facets of the one soul. There is no reason to suppose that this process will not go on forever, repeating itself in the souls that are added to them.

Leroy's astral visits continued, with one difference. Formerly his astral travels had happened mainly in his sleep; now he had learned to direct his spirit body consciously, feeling himself to be a shaft of light, pointed where he willed. It was a high-consciousness experience for him as well as for Alexandra.

From time to time they met in person in various parts of the world. Then it was as though they had never been apart. And indeed, when they were apart, they felt the oneness of spirit more keenly than when face-to-face. In their meetings they refrained from sexual relations, intuitively sensing that the body would be an encumbrance. The truth was they had progressed beyond the physical in their expressions of love. They now knew that what people yearn for in the joinings of the flesh is the complete union that is possible only to spirit bodies.

⤚

The raising of sexual energy from the physical to the higher levels of the spirit is not yet an experience that many have had, but we believe it is written on the future. As spiritual advancements continue there will be spirit-sexual meetings and experiences of bliss in many refined and subtle ways. Yet it is also true that an instinct must be fully explored and satiated before it can be left behind. The idea of prematurely forcing an ascension of the sexual drive to unnatural celibacy amounts to nothing more than repression, the antithesis of growth.

Alexandra and Leroy's reach to each other and their breakthrough into spiritual dimensions is an example of human capacity extended beyond itself. They didn't know their capacity until they were tested. Every human being has vast resources as yet unrealized, ready to be unlocked by the power of love, awakening the many levels of the spirit. Coiled within each of us is the kundalini power, which, when released, will gather all the body-spirit forces into one fused and blended stream of energy. This was the energy directed toward Alexandra by her twin and actively received by her. The infusion of power, transmitted to her repeatedly across vast geographical distances, caused her etheric body to intensify its vitality, and the physical body to be galvanized and energized. Her entire aura was coordinated and illumined, allowing her spirit form to withdraw in full waking consciousness and unite with Leroy's in the pure and sacred lovemaking of the higher planes.

This is sexual energy in its transcendent expression,

the one force manifesting in all forms, and expressing as love: love between twin souls, and the love intention between doctor and patient, parent and child, teacher and pupil, friend and friend. It is the energy that keeps the stars and planets in their places while continually expanding their reach toward the limitless. It is the high mirroring of our own expanding love.

Spiritual lovemaking is the union of body and soul natural to this new age of synthesis. With the deepening dimensions in our outlook we can see the broad applications of sex transcendence. It can be expressed in loving sexual intercourse, which allows the spirit full involvement; or between a departed spirit and a loved one on this earth; or, as we have seen in the bridge constructed between Alexandra and her twin, between the spirits of two living mortals.

It is a bridge that many others will construct. As time goes on, there will be a flowing traffic between the worlds, or through the spaces of this world, empowering lovers in all circumstances, those held apart by distance, by physical infirmity, or by the illusory separation we call death.

A word of warning: there have been reports of spirit-sex encounters in some books on astral travel, but its dangers are seldom mentioned. To project oneself out into the astral world looking for love is rather like walking naked down a dark alley late at night. The astral air is crowded with spirits untrustworthy and even dangerous. For your safety you must have a focus for your projection: a person known in this life, or a beloved partner who has passed over to the other side. Two people with established bonds of love, if spiritually developed, will be able to span the worlds and unite their spirits in acts of love. No doubt it has been happening through the ages, in dreams or the unconsciousness of sleep, and goes largely unrecognized. These ideas are not new. They are at least as old as Greek mythology, foreshadowed in the love between gods and humans.

Humans and gods are drawing closer with the present speeding-up of evolution. By gods we mean the advanced spiritual beings who guide our destiny, and the godlike qualities in the self. Together these draw us closer to recognizing the ultimate bridge between life and death. We have crossed it many times, in sleep, in the little death of love's ecstasy, in our banishment from the true home and helpless awakening to this world at birth.

And finally, on the day of the glad return, the life-purpose fulfilled, the body will be left behind.

Eva Pierrakos leads us back across the bridge:

> Though the body will be transcended and cease to exist, it is not true that the feelings you experience

in an unblocked body and soul condition while in the body will also cease to exist. The opposite is true: the body feelings come from the subtle bodies. Thus, when bodily existence is transcended, those identical feelings will manifest much more strongly, because they will not be blocked by the gross matter of physical existence. The feelings of pleasure and bliss which you registered in your body will not cease to exist in an existence beyond the earth life. They will be intensified. You will be more capable of sustaining the feelings of pleasure supreme, ecstasy, bliss, love and what is called sexuality on this earth.

8 Twin Souls in History

TWIN SOULS HAVE BEEN MEETING, JOINING, AND serving the world throughout history. Most have contributed anonymously, as they do now; but some, as now, have risen to prominence.

In the following pages we will examine a few of the marriages between lovers rich in accomplishment and marked with the distinguishing signs of twinsoulship. Such heroic twin-soul lovers are an inspiration to us all. They are models for everyone, for the future near and distant, a future that is racing toward us.

Elizabeth Barrett and Robert Browning

Elizabeth Barrett and Robert Browning came together in mid-nineteenth-century London when Robert wrote to Elizabeth praising her work. Elizabeth was already renowned as a poet. It would be twenty years before Robert would achieve comparable fame. She, six years older, perceived the work of his struggling youth as superior to hers; throughout their lives each would insist that the other was the greater poet.

Their correspondence, as well, became a major contribution to literature. It was prodigious—573 letters survive—making their correspondence one of the longest, fullest, and most self-contained in English literary history. Elizabeth Barrett was a semi-invalid, virtually a prisoner of her despotic father in their home on Wimpole Street. Her only companions were her sisters, her brothers, and her books. As for courtship and marriage, she wrote of the senior Barrett: "He would sooner see me dead at his feet than belong to another."

Robert Browning courted her nonetheless, and she responded. Their incessant letter writing took the place of personal encounters, though Robert made many afternoon visits to Wimpole Street when Barrett senior was at his office. Miraculously, Elizabeth gained in strength. She had scarcely been able to move about her room but now began venturing out to Regent's Park with her maid, Wilson, first in a wheelchair and soon on foot. Through the power of love she overcame her physical frailty, then dared to take her life into her own hands and entrust it to Robert.

As reports of Robert Browning's visits reached him, the elder Barrett swiftly made arrangements to move his family out of London. It became necessary for the lovers to act. On a September morning in 1846,

Elizabeth left the house with Wilson, ostensibly to visit an old teacher. They took a cab the short distance to Saint Marylebone Church, where Elizabeth and Robert were married. One week later they secretly eloped to Italy, where they made their home, continued their writings, and eventually produced a son. Elizabeth's father returned all her letters unopened and did not permit her name to be spoken again in his house.

In all the great love stories of life, literature, and opera the theme of dark-force opposition appears. Evil finds a powerful avenue in parental jealousy and possessiveness. Parental opposition provided the tragedy of *Romeo and Juliet*. But the Brownings' story had a happy ending, and furthermore, the opposition that restricted their courtship meetings gave us the permanent gift of their love letters to each other.

The gender balance of the two poets stands out clearly, constantly reiterated in statements made by and about them. Describing Robert in a letter, Elizabeth wrote: "The intellect is little in comparison to all the rest—to the womanly tenderness, the inexhaustible goodness, the high and noble aspiration of every hour. Temper, spirits, manners—there is not a flaw anywhere."

To Robert himself, she wrote: "You are 'masculine' to the height—and I, as a woman, have studied some of your gestures of language and intonation wistfully, as a thing beyond me far! and the more admirable for being beyond."

We see Browning as an embodiment of the evolved masculine soul, his "womanly tenderness" in balance and blend with his strengths. Osbert Burdett, his biographer, gives a capsule description of Browning when he says of the letters, "Except in their sincerity his are the exact opposite of hers. Grace, vividness, charm are not the qualities of his side of their correspondence. His letters are rugged and rough and tender and patient and considerate and strong."

Of Elizabeth, Burdett writes: "In the best of her work, as in her life, she was his complement, but unlike some women of genius she was wholly feminine. . . . One is inclined to say that with any other husband she would have collapsed. The love that never fails was his. . . . The dream that is so often indulged, so rarely realized, was fulfilled for this pair, and it is idle to attempt to communicate their possession. It makes us realize afresh how exceptional is such mutual affection, how rare a marriage like this."

The biographer with no conscious knowledge of the twinship of souls is often its best exponent, for he or she speaks without bias.

> Both poets make us realize the beauty of character, and it may be said of her [Barrett], as she said of

Browning, that the least important part about him was his genius. . . . In Browning we take the genius for granted, and can look at the man, and the man proves a revelation. . . . The fact is that he was whole.

As a man and artist he was masculine to the core. . . . He had an immense capacity for affection, and this capacity was equalled by his wife. The only circumstance that hit him to the heart was her death when both were middle-aged. . . . The great question of what lay beyond the world was bound up for him with the loss of his wife. When death took her away, the centre of his being hung in the balance, and his inner life was ruled by hope and fear for nearly thirty years after she died.

She was as nearly his religion as one person can be to another. . . . They possessed the experience [of love] as rare in fact as it is in fiction. It survived every test. He was thirty-three before he became engaged; he was a husband for fifteen years; he lived for twenty-eight years a widower. There was only one love in his life, and only one in hers. Despite all the conventions to the contrary, this is a strange and wonderful thing. Among love stories it is a fairy tale, and it is true.

That two human beings capable of this experience should realize it together is exceptional; that both should be poets is doubly strange. In their life and in their work they were the complementary opposites of one another. She was feminine to the marrow, and only became a complete poet when she put her women's response to his love into verse.

Perhaps we may sum up their relation by saying that she was that which Shelley had promised, but failed to remain: a lyric poet of love "showing the correspondency of the natural to the spiritual," a human being "tender and sincere," who, through her capacity for love, radiated something of divine power and influence.

As a lyric poet of love, Elizabeth Barrett Browning still speaks to us through her immortal sonnet to Robert:

> How do I love thee? Let me count the ways.
> I love thee to the depth and breadth and height
> My soul can reach, when feeling out of sight
> For the ends of Being and ideal Grace.
> I love thee to the level of every day's
> Most quiet need, by sun and candle-light.
> I love thee freely, as men strive for Right;
> I love thee purely, as they turn from Praise.
> I love thee with the passion put to use
> In my old griefs, and with my childhood's faith.
> I love thee with a love I seemed to lose
> With my lost saints—I love thee with the breadth,
> Smiles, tears of all my life—and, if God choose,
> I shall but love thee better after death.

Marie and Pierre Curie

If the Brownings radiated to the world a divine power through their art, the gift was paralleled in science by Pierre Curie, the French physicist, and his Polish wife, Marie. The Curies were married in Paris in 1895, and in 1903 jointly received the Nobel Prize for their discovery of radium. Their work with radioactivity finally forced a reconsideration of the foundation of physics and chemistry.

The Curies' marriage was as close to perfection as this earth allows. Of Pierre, Marie wrote: "I have the best husband one could dream of; I could never have imagined finding one like him. He is a true gift of heaven, and the more we live together the more we love each other."

The yin intuitive faculty played a large part in the Curies' destiny, for at first Marie only guessed at the possible existence of the new element radium. To prove its existence she used her highly evolved yang strength and determination in a physical and mental labor that would have exhausted anyone else. The radium had to be extracted from pitchblende in an interminably slow process, one ton of pitchblende yielding a mere one-tenth gram of radium chloride in the early experiments. Pierre aided her in this work in a spirit of protectiveness and support, which is wholly masculine. At the same time he showed the yin qualities that enabled him to share the management of a home and children while leading a life dedicated to scientific pursuit.

Their life together was shattered suddenly and tragically, on April 19, 1906, when Pierre was run over by a cart on the rue Dauphine in Paris and instantly killed. Marie went on with her life in science and continued to care for her two daughters, the older of whom would later win a Nobel Prize of her own. In 1909 Marie was named to her husband's chair in physics at the Sorbonne, and in 1911 she was awarded a Nobel Prize for her isolation of radium and her studies in chemistry.

Their younger daughter, Eve, in her biography of her mother, *Madame Curie*, gives us the distinctive twin-soul description:

> The two souls, like the two brains, were of equal quality. They formed one of the finest bonds that ever united man and woman. Two hearts beat together, two bodies were united, and two minds of genius learned to think together. Marie could have married no other than this great physicist, than this wise and noble man; Pierre could have married no woman other than the fair, tender Polish girl, who could be childish or transcendent within the same few moments; for she was a friend and a wife, a lover and a scientist.

Marie never remarried, nor did Robert Browning after the loss of Elizabeth. It is safe to suppose that these four souls came into incarnation prepared for the twin union. Readiness comes when sexual trial and learning have been completed—possibly in previous lives.

Even though they did not know one another, we could imagine the Brownings and the Curies occupying adjacent positions in the group soul. The two couples would then have been next-of-twin. Next-of-twin couples will most probably complement each other in mentality, each pair representing one of the two great streams of human endeavor, art or science.

Art and science could be thought of respectively as the yin and yang of mentalities, each with contramentality present, in the same pattern as the opposite genders. As the highly evolved man is developed also in his feminine aspects, the highly evolved scientist is likely to be a burgeoning artist. Einstein played the violin; Churchill, that great political scientist, became a noted painter. Perhaps the most outstanding example of an artistic mentality with scientific powers is Leonardo da Vinci, who sketched the submarine, the airplane, and, alas, the machine gun, long before they were invented. Da Vinci showed that at a very high stage of evolvement the complementary mental streams can become virtually equal. We can expect the same with the opposite genders.

But before then, there is much evolving to be done and opposition to be met. Like the Brownings, the Curies attracted the force that resists advancement, this time from the scientific establishment. Yet despite all opposition, both couples were able to fight through and realize the promise of their lives and their work. History so rarely portrays this fulfillment of great love and high achievement that we are left to wonder how many twin souls have been intercepted at the point of union, and how much noble work intended for the world has failed to be born.

Héloïse and Abélard

One of the most vivid twin-soul tragedies is the story of the twelfth-century lovers Abélard and Héloïse. Peter Abélard was a French philosopher and theologian, a brilliant teacher and dialectician, as well as a leading figure in medieval scholasticism. Héloïse was the niece of a canon. Her love affair with Abélard resulted in the birth of a child and a subsequent secret marriage. Héloïse's uncle took revenge on Abélard by having him kidnapped and emasculated.

Following this cruel punishment, Abélard entered religious life. Long afterward he could write of it to Héloïse as an act of God's mercy that rid him of the torments of the flesh. But what he vividly recalls in his *Historia* is the pain and horror, his feelings of humiliation and disgust at being a eunuch, the unclean beast of Jewish law. He admits that "it was shame and confusion in my remorse and misery rather than any devout wish for conversion which brought me to seek shelter in a monastery cloister."

Héloïse, following the pattern of their shared destiny, joined the Benedictine order of nuns and would later become Mother Superior of the convent of the Paraclete, established by Abélard. It is believed that their famous letters were exchanged at this period. Their love has cast a light across the centuries, providing material for works of tragic literature even to this day.

Their service to the dark and superstitious world of their time did not come without tremendous cost. The pain of their forced separation was a wound that had no healing in their lifetime. Héloïse's pain is poured out in her letters:

> The pleasures of lovers which we shared . . . can scarcely be banished from my thoughts. Wherever I turn they are always there before my eyes, bringing with them awakened longings and fantasies which will not even let me sleep. Even during the celebration of the Mass, where our prayers should be purer, lewd visions of those pleasures take such

a hold upon my unhappy soul that my thoughts are on their wantonness instead of on prayers. I should be groaning over the sins I have committed, but I can only sigh for what I have lost. Everything we did and also the times and places are stamped on my heart along with your image, so that I live through it all again with you. Even in sleep I know no respite. Sometimes my thoughts are betrayed in a movement of my body, or they break out in an unguarded word. In my utter wretchedness, that cry from a suffering soul could well be mine: "Miserable creature that I am, who is there to rescue me out of the body doomed to this death?" Would that in truth I could go on: "The grace of God through Jesus Christ our Lord." This grace, my dearest, came upon you unsought—a single wound of the body by freeing you from these torments has healed many wounds in your soul. . . . But for me, youth and passion and experience of pleasures which were so delightful intensify the torments of the flesh and longings of desire, and the assault is the more overwhelming as the nature they attack is the weaker. Men call me chaste; they do not know the hypocrite I am. They consider purity of the flesh a virtue, though virtue belongs not to the body but to the soul.

Abélard responds to her from his intellect and his place of priestly detachment:

When I am suffering in despair of my life, would
it be fitting for you to be joyous? Would you want
to be partners only in joy, not grief, to join in re-
joicing without weeping with those who weep? . . .
I come at last to your old perpetual complaint, in
which you presume to blame God for the manner
of our entry into religion instead of wishing to
glorify him as you justly should. . . . Remember
what you have said, recall what you have written,
namely that in the manner of our conversion,
when God seems to have been more my adversary,
he had clearly shown himself kinder. . . . You
should not grieve because you are the cause of
so great a good, for which you must not doubt
you were specially created by God. . . . See then,
my beloved, see how with the dragnets of his
mercy the Lord has fished us up from the depths
of this dangerous sea, although we were unwilling,
so that each of us may justly break out in that cry:
"The Lord takes thought for me.". . . Comfort
by our example any unrighteous who despair of
God's goodness, so that all may know what may
be done for those who ask with prayer, when such
benefits are granted sinners even against their
will.

There can be little doubt that the tragedy of these
lovers was the work of separative forces, though ultimately, as always, the results were to serve a higher

purpose. Part of that purpose was to bring their love story to the forefront of human legend.

Clara and Robert Schumann

The great nineteenth-century German composer Robert Schumann was an established concert pianist when he met the nine-year-old Clara. She was already a virtuoso at the keyboard and destined to become the most celebrated woman pianist of her time. They fell in love gradually, as Schumann watched a delightful, gifted child blossom into a beautiful young woman. He proposed marriage when she was fifteen.

Here the opposition took the same form as with Elizabeth Barrett: a consuming and possessive father. Clara's father, the noted piano teacher Friedrich Wieck, refused to allow the marriage and tried in every way to stop the love that was developing between his daughter and Robert Schumann. Three years later the lovers went to court to force his consent to their marriage.

The marriage took place in 1840, whereupon Schumann literally burst into song. The year 1840 has been called "the song year," with one masterpiece following another. The year 1841 was "the symphony year," and 1842 "the chamber music year." It was as though Schumann knew that something evil was pursuing him—as it was. Long haunted by fear of insanity, he had made suicide attempts earlier in his life. The years of happiness with Clara were short. By the late 1840s Schumann was suffering increasingly from bouts of mental illness. Periods of depression began to affect his work. Although he produced a number of masterpieces, among them the Piano Concerto in A Minor, many compositions were begun and never finished.

Early in 1854, Schumann recorded in his diary a painful aural symptom, the sound of a single note that never stopped, sometimes turning into chords and the strains of a full orchestra. At times the music was "more wonderful and played by more exquisite instruments than ever sounded on earth," such as on the night when he got out of bed to note down a theme brought him by the angels from Schubert and Mendelssohn.

At other times it was a cacophony of hyenas and demon voices, goading him to such desperation and despair that at night he begged Clara to leave him for fear that he might harm her.

Clara noted in her diary: "If I so much as touched him, he said, 'Ah! Clara, I am not worthy of your love.' *He* said this, he whom I always look up to with the greatest, the most profound reverence." It proved to be the most traumatic day of her life: for on that night, in his anguish, Schumann fled the house in a heavy rain and threw himself into the Rhine. Fishermen rescued him, but he knew that his lifelong dread had turned to hideous reality. He asked to be taken to a lunatic asylum, and he was committed to a private asylum at Endenich. Later he was able to correspond with Clara, and with Johannes Brahms, who was a close friend. He was never allowed to see Clara; she was told that there was no hope of recovery.

Clara knew that Brahms's loyalty to the lonely sufferer at Endenich was as rocklike as her own, even as the depth of his devotion to her became unmistakable. During the two and a half years of Robert's incarceration, she was obliged to continue with concert tours in order to support their children. Brahms's letters were her lifeline, keeping her informed of her children's development and conveying what little news he could of Schumann's state. He wrote nearly every day, addressing her as "My dearly beloved Clara," and not attempting to disguise the fact that she had become the center of his life. "I can no longer exist without you," he confessed. "Please go on loving me as I shall go on loving you, always and forever."

Obviously Brahms had fallen deeply in love with Clara. These three undoubtedly belonged to the great musical group soul incarnated at that period. Group-soul love has very specific purposes, such as in this instance the devotion, consolation, and support that Brahms was able to give Clara in the absence of her twin.

Here we are shown the depth of group-soul love,

differing only in degree from the love of twins. Clara was Brahms's substitute for his twin. He had elected to work alone on this earth, for reasons known only to his soul, while the Schumanns had chosen to incarnate together. They all paid a price in suffering; but the great musical works were given to the world by group assent. Brahms's inspiring spirit may have been his twin, as might Beethoven's, for the "immortal beloved" was never identified among the women the composer knew and disastrously loved.

As the end drew near for Schumann, Clara pleaded with his doctors to be allowed to see him. Returning with Brahms, she demanded one last reunion, and it was granted.

Her diary records: "He smiled and put his arm around me with a great effort, for he can no longer control his limbs. I shall never forget it. Not all the treasures in the world could equal this embrace." And later: "Two and a half years ago you were torn from me without any farewell, though your heart must have been full, and now I lay silent at your feet hardly daring to breathe; only now and then I received a look, clouded as it were, but unspeakably gentle. . . . Everything about him was holy to me, even the air which he, my noble husband, breathed with me. He seemed to speak much with spirit."

Release came the following evening. "I stood by the

body of my passionately loved husband, and was calm. All my feelings were absorbed in thankfulness to God that he was at last set free, and as I knelt by his bed I was filled with awe, it was as if his holy spirit was hovering over me—Ah! If only he had taken me with him. I laid some flowers on his head—my love, he has taken with him. . . . God, give me the strength to live without him. . . . With his departure, all my happiness is over."

Though he begged her to do so, she refused to marry Brahms.

Harriet Taylor and John Stuart Mill

One of the happiest recorded twin-soul histories is that of John Stuart Mill and Harriet Taylor, who met in London at the end of the 1820s. Harriet was a brilliant young woman, unhappily married to a man who was kindly but very much her intellectual inferior. Her misery at the empty companionship and the stultification of her faculties finally led her to seek the counsel of her Unitarian minister, William Johnson Fox. This remarkable man took seriously her desire for intellectual stimulation and companionship. He offered to introduce her to John Stuart Mill.

Mill, soon to be recognized as the foremost social thinker of his time, had already achieved renown with his essay *The Spirit of the Age.* He was twenty-four, a year older than Harriet, and his need was as great as hers. Despite his brilliance he had sunk deep into depression, yearning for the "great joy and happiness" that seemed to elude him, feeling as if he had "nothing left to live for."

He was to discover, in finding Harriet Taylor, that he had *everything* to live for. He later wrote:

> I had always wished for a friend whom I could admire wholly, without reservation and restriction, and now I had found one. To render this possible it was necessary that the object of my admiration should be of a type different from my own; should be a character predominantly of feeling, combined however, as I had not in any other instance known it to be, with a vigorous and bold speculative intellect.

Very soon after their meeting, he and Harriet were deeply involved, writing essays together, seeing each other daily, and exchanging fervent letters. Almost at a stroke, they made the leap to the gender balance that defines the twin souls. Their intellects matched, and their two dispositions complemented each other. Where he was careful, she was daring; where he was detached and balanced, she was partial and intuitive. Mill felt as though another world had been opened to him. He had always pursued the good and the true, but without drawing upon his deepest vitality. This was what he had missed in his arid intellectualism: beauty and passion.

Harriet candidly faced her husband with her feelings for Mill. John Taylor asked her to forgo seeing Mill, but she could not do without her friend, and her husband could not bear to see her unhappy. Gradually Mill was sanctioned in the role of platonic lover and visited the Taylors' house every night of the week. The personal ethics of Harriet and Mill demanded that they ask the question: How is the greatest quantity of unhappiness to be avoided? They decided that the least unhappiness would result from Harriet's staying with Taylor, provided she could continue to enjoy the company of Mill.

In the more than twenty years that passed before they were free to marry they produced all the major works that bear Mill's name but that he declared were joint productions. He wrote: "Not only during the years of our married life, but during many years of confidential friendship which preceded it, all my published writings are as much my wife's work as mine." They include: *Principles of Political Economy, On Liberty, The Autobiography, The Subjection of Women,* and the numerous essays on religion, all of which had been discussed, drafted, planned, and in some cases dictated by Harriet.

On the death of John Taylor, Harriet and Mill

scarcely felt the need to marry, so closely were their minds and souls already wedded. They submitted to a marriage ceremony only so that they could live under the same roof and not waste the time traveling to each other daily. They took a secluded house and were supremely happy, discussing everything, sharing everything, dedicated to their writing. Neither had any interest in the artificial pleasures of society, for they found each other absolutely fascinating, and the fascination never dimmed.

There is in twin souls a certain obedience to each other, not unlike the mystic's obedience to God. While standing strong within themselves, they are quick to defer to each other, from a deeply felt sense that the other is in a way their best self. This sense was particularly marked in John Stuart Mill. He wrote at Harriet's direction, saying once, typically, "I want my angel to tell me what should be the next essay written."

His mind was one of the amazing phenomena of the age; his skull is reported to have contained the largest brain known to science yet the feeling part of himself, which he needed to mobilize thought, dwelled in Harriet. He wrote to her: "What would be the use of my outliving you! I could write nothing worth keeping alive except with your prompting."

Some biographers believe that the Mills' relationship may have been nonsexual. Harriet had stopped having sexual intercourse with her husband after meeting Mill, and she may have decided to give up sex altogether. But if their relationship was nonsexual, there could be another explanation. This supremely mated pair may have transcended physical love, discovering that when the pleasures of the body are renounced, sexuality rises to higher levels of consciousness where all the excitement and lovingness of ordinary sexuality take on a finer edge.

We can be certain that their sexual energies were well and fully used, their masculine and feminine forces flowing into each other in the free exchange of the completed, androgynous being. Her intellect flowered, and his feeling self came into its own. Devoted to the service of humanity, rich in love for each other, they employed their matching talents in a single focus that had profound influence on the time.

Seven years after their marriage, Harriet died in France. Mill bought a house overlooking the French cemetery where she was buried. He spent more and more time there every year, and while in England he continued their work, knowing that she still guided his life.

His great consolation was Harriet's twenty-seven-year-old daughter, Helen Taylor, who became his companion for the rest of his life. "Surely," he wrote, "no one ever before was so fortunate as, after a loss such

as mine, to draw another prize in the lottery of life—
another companion, stimulator, advisor, and instructor
of the rarest quality."

His love had a focus again and was able to express itself in a continued life of devotion. This was not a lottery prize he'd won but a gift from the Divine Plan. We
can be confident that Helen came to him from a near
position in his and Harriet's group soul, just as Brahms
was there to console Clara Schumann in her loss.

How significant it is that the man who led the
thinkers of his generation possessed such a feminine
love nature. He epitomizes the high level of the feminine in the evolved masculine soul. It is truly masculine
to love greatly and have the courage to say so.

Petrarch and Laura

Only a poet can fully express in words the high love
of the soul. Early among these was Petrarch, the
fourteenth-century poet laureate of Italy, whose sonnets to Laura are considered the greatest love poems
ever written.

Petrarch writes: "Laura, illustrious by her own virtues and long celebrated in my poems, first appeared to
my eyes in the earliest period of my manhood on the
sixth day of April, anno Domini 1327, in the Church of
St. Claire at Avignon, at the morning hour. And in the
same city at the same hour of the same day in the same

month of April, but in the year 1348, that light was withdrawn from our day."

From his first sight of her until her death from the black plague twenty-one years later she was the focusing passion of his life:

> I have never been weary of this love,
> My lady, nor shall I be while last my years.

In the final collection of Petrarch's verse were 366 poems, known in Italian by the generic name *Rime.* The theme of the overwhelming majority of the *Rime* is his love for Laura, "in life and in death." The collection is divided into two parts, the first containing the poems written *"In vita di Madonna Laura,"* the second, *"In morté di Madonna Laura."*

Historians believe that Laura was the daughter of a Provençal nobleman, Audibert de Noves, and married to Hugues de Sade. She mothered many children— some say eleven. That Petrarch's love for Laura was denied fulfillment in the usual sense set the tone for his sonnets and songs. Above all, the *Rime* sings of the sad and woeful beauty of love, of the longing for the unattainable, of the rebellion against denial, of the inward laceration of the lover, and of his melancholic resignation. In the *Rime* all these moods of a lover have found their timeless representation. And the very fact that the figure of Laura is so idealized has made it possible for many readers of these sonnets to see in the image of Laura the picture of their own beloved, and to hear in the words of the poet the expression of their own thoughts and the echoes of their own love.

This may well have been the higher purpose in the arrangement that held these twin souls apart, if twins they were. If they were, we would expect to see a matching poetic gift in Laura; but the poetic talents of women were not publicly expressed in those times. Still, twins might incarnate expressly for one to inspire the other to great heights of artistry, for their own evolutionary benefit and that of the world—in this case to give utterance to the mute longings of so many through the centuries. Or again, Laura may not have been his twin but one a little more removed in the group soul who struck a resonance within him that brought forth the passion for the absent twin, known to him in spiritual heights.

We do see repeated here the familiar twin pattern of attributing the best of oneself to one's counterpart. Petrarch wrote: "Whatever little I am, I have become through her. For if I possess any name and fame at all, I should never have obtained them unless she had cared with her most noble affection for the sparse seeds of virtues planted in my bosom by Nature."

"Laura's mind," he continues, "does not know earthly cares but burns with heavenly desires. Her appearance truly radiates beams of divine beauty. Her morals are an example of perfect uprightness. Neither her voice nor the force of her eyes nor her gait are those of an ordinary human being."

Petrarch asserted emphatically that he had "always loved her soul more than her body," though he admitted that, under the compulsion of love and youth, "occasionally I wished something dishonorable."

Eventually Petrarch succeeded in conquering himself, for he writes in the *Secretum,* composed in the form of a dialogue between himself and Saint Augustine, his spiritual guide and conscience: "Now I know what I want and wish, and my unstable mind has become firm. She, on her part, has always been steadfast and has always stayed one and the same. The better I understand her womanly constancy, the more I admire it. If once I was grieved by her unyielding resolution, I am now full of joy over it and thankful."

In a later sonnet he expresses his profound gratitude:

> I thank her soul and her holy device
> That with her face and her sweet anger's bolts
> Bid me in burning think of my salvation.

The climax of this love story is reached when Petrarch, inspired by the example of Laura's perfection, masters himself and his desires and begins to strive for the salvation of his soul. Eventually Laura assumes an ideal nature, as disclosed in one of the sonnets:

> In what part of the sky, in what idea
> Was the example from which Nature wrought
> That charming lovely face wherein she sought
> To show her power in the upper sphere?

This conception of Laura as the sublime ideal shows most clearly the transformation that Laura had undergone in the poet's mind: she has become the image of the concept of beauty, the embodiment of good and right. His perception of Laura's ultimate transfiguration is revealed in a later sonnet where his

> inner eye
> Sees her soar up and with the angels fly
> At the feet of our own eternal Lord.

His last, great unfinished work, the *Canzoniere*, is a symbolic vision of one man's story, raised from the autobiographical to the universal, the story of humanity in its progress from earthly passion to fulfillment in God. Love triumphs over the greatest men, but is captured by Chastity; which in its turn, in the person of Laura, is overcome by Death; which is conquered by glory, which is itself annihilated by Time:

only in God does everything of beauty and everything of value, love for Laura and for glory, shine eternally beyond all space and time, and heaven and earth are reconciled according to Petrarch's noble and constant dream.

Lilian Steichen and Carl Sandburg

A more contemporary poet, Carl Sandburg, celebrates soul-love in his poems and letters to his wife, Lilian Steichen. Born in 1878, Sandburg would become revered as one of American's greatest poets. *A Great and Glorious Romance* is the title given by Helga Sandburg to her biography of her parents, published in 1978. Their marriage was a love affair that endured through a long life together of creativity and family harmony.

Carl's and Lilian's letters and the many poems he dedicated to her speak the language of twinship. In an early poem he writes:

> Woman of a million names and a thousand faces,
> I looked for you over the earth and under the sky.
> I sought you in passing processions
> On old multitudinous highways
> Where mask and phantom and life go by.
> In roaming and roving, from prairies to sea,
> From city to wilderness, fighting and praying,
> I looked.

When I saw you, I knew you as you knew me.
We knew we had known far back in the eons
When hills were a dust and the sea a mist.
And toil is a trifle and struggle a glory
With You, and ruin and death but fancies,
Woman of a million names and a thousand faces.

In Carl's letters to Lilian he refers to their union as
the S-S. "The S-S stands for two Souls. The hyphen
means they have met and are. S-S stands for *poise.* It
means intensity and vibration and radiation, but over
and above these are harmony and equilibrium. . . . The
great fact is *we have met— YOU ARE!!!"*

It is natural for lovers everywhere to marvel at the
fact of their meeting. With twin souls the wonder is
amplified. At that point in their evolution, they are
fated only for each other; no one else will do; they have
been through all the practice loves. What a miracle it
seems, then, that the two of them should arrive on the
pinpoint, as it were, of destiny!

Lilian expresses her feelings in no less degree:

My heart so yearning to you! . . . What a Glory
that the Soul should be so transfused into the
Body! The Body no more a Hulk—no more a
thing of Wood—but etherialized—a Speaking
Flame! What a consecration! A realist Pentecost!

Their exultation knew no limits. Carl writes in an early letter:

> All my life I must write at this letter — this Letter
> of Love to the Great Woman Who Came and
> Knew and Loved. All my life this must go on! The
> Idea and the Emotion are so vast it will be years
> and years in issuing. Ten thousand lovebirds, sweet
> throated and red-plumed, were in my soul, in the
> garden of my under-life. There on ten thousand
> branches they slept as in night-time. You came and
> they awoke. For a moment they fluttered distract-
> edly in joy at stars and odors and breezes. And
> a dawn burst on them — a long night was ended.
> God! how they sang. God! The music of those
> throats — such dulcets and diapasons of song they
> sang! I hear them and I know them. These birds
> want freedom. These imprisoned songsters are all
> to be loosed. But I can only let out one at a time.
> Each letter, then, is some joy till now jailed — but
> now sent flying: — at the touch of release, called
> out by the Woman who came. — And we will fling
> the world twenty-thousand beautiful, vibrating,
> fleeting, indomitable, happy love-birds singing
> love-songs swelling the world's joy.

The love utterances of poets may seem exaggerated
to the undiscerning eye but are true reflections of the
spirit in its unveiled glory. When two poets express the

reciprocal love of matching souls they light up the way before us. This is their mission on the earth, as well as the fulfillment of their own ageless search.

These two had been following conjoined paths of poetry long before they met. They were steeped in a love for the same poets: Keats, Shelley, Browning, Whitman, Carpenter. They spoke the same language. Their literary tastes had matured, as their love was matured before they set eyes on each other.

Lilian's poetic talent reflects his, as she writes:

Have I really some part in your human poems? This thought fills me with such sweet wonder and hope. I have been conscious in rare poignant moments in my life of something very beautiful deep deep within me, but the Voice from those depths has always been so small, so still—more a *hush* than a *voice*—that I never dreamed that anyone but myself would hear it. But so finely attuned was that heart of yours, you caught the fine vibrant note from the depths—and . . . gave it strength and quality. In your poems somehow (I dare *hope*— believe it!) the sweet still hush of my heart has become blended with the clear strong proud Music of yours and so is heard! It is heard—and the farthest star and the last son of man will vibrate to it. But for you, the sweet small hush yearning upward toward light and utterance would have

subsided back to the dark depths—subsided and
subsided—till it lost what small strength for upward yearning it had—and so died forever! So glad
thanks to you—for Voice! for Life!

Not only in their poetic gifts but in all else the
Sandburgs present a picture of twin-soul synchronic-
ity and complementary balance. In that most important
area of spiritual belief, they both recognized a universal
religion of humanism and joy-in-life, a religion common to all, to those who accept theologies and to those
who have no theology. Both were also political beings,
a rare thing among poets. Carl's masterwork was his biography of Lincoln, originally published in six volumes.
He also lectured and campaigned for the Socialists.
"Back of the great love must be great action," he wrote,
and during World War I was a correspondent in
Sweden.

In Lilian Steichen he found the same breadth of
mind, the same reach of the soul toward betterment
of society and self. He wrote to her: "The coincidence
of our ideas and plans and whims is something I would
not have believed till the Wonder-Woman came!"

Lilian was clear about her course. When her brother,
the photographer Edward Steichen, urged her to make
full use of her writing powers, she responded: "I am
content to be, instead of a genius, an average human

being. There's wonder and joy enough in being a mere human being—a Woman!"

Her daughter tells us:

I have always known her as totally female; her power over my father was continuous and subtle. There never were loud arguments back and forth in our house. My father raged and roared, and often. But she coaxed him out of it. When he was very old, I saw them standing in the kitchen together. He had pulled at a door handle which stuck. He rattled it and shouted. A small woman, she looked up at him and patted his chest. "What a fine strong voice!" Disarmed, he stood there in love. It was a thread established early and woven through their life.

Referring to her father's travels, Helga Sandburg writes: "Viewing my parents these many years later and studying their lives, it always helps that when they were apart and restless they wrote of love and news back and forth. Whenever they settled together for a while, comfortable, my contact with them stops." And so does ours. We may thank the travels, then, as the occasion for the great love letters.

On one of his lecture tours he found time to

sit by a riverside under trees and starlight and think about this wonder and glory of You-Me-

the-S-S. . . . You are with me always as a redeeming,
transcending Presence. (You posed for Titian—
I was marauding on a Viking ship but I missed
you then—That was why I kept on marauding!)
Always you are with me, giving me your smile for
my failures and mistakes, accepting everything,
having seen in me as I have seen in you—a something last and final of sacred resolve and conse-
crated desire—the something that gave us each a
Tint of silver in our youths—by which each inter-
prets all that the other does, always seeing *intentions*
if not accomplishments. . . . No poem, nor biogra-
phies will ever analyze or depict the S-S!

She responds with the same exultancy and poetic
vigor—the one soul, speaking back and forth within
itself:

Such letters, Heart, such letters! What a Man you
are! You are the Miracle that I have looked and
looked for all these years! The Miracle has come to
pass . . . lo—the Ideal become Real! *You to love* . . .
surely I am blest among women. . . . After a while
will come a beautiful calm acceptance of the S-S,
something really grander than this present exclama-
tory ecstasy! . . .

   The World has created us and has brought us
together: it has produced the atoms and has given

them to chance to unite in the S-S molecule! Our
first duty is to appreciate this gift of Nature's.
It has cost eons of agony and toil and blunders
to fashion and shape our two atoms. And for
eons Nature has sought to bring these two atoms
together—but always we just missed each other
and Nature was baffled for the time! Now she has
achieved her purpose: *The S-S molecule is!* . . . We will
give the S-S the best chance! . . . And then to do
what service we can for Society!

The theme of service appears frequently here, as always with the union of souls. And where twin souls
unite, we needn't look far to see others of the group
gathering near or perhaps already linked in earth-
family connection. We believe this to have been the case
with Lilian and Edward Steichen, a sister and brother
bonded in extraordinary closeness through their childhood and adult lives. Added to this is the affection that
flowered spontaneously between Edward and Carl in
the way of group souls, possessed of equal and similar
artistic powers.

Together they demonstrate the soul-family, each
with its mission for humanity, wise in the ways of love,
predictive of future families on earth as they reflect in
harmony and joy the shared radiance of their related
souls.

The Mother and Sri Aurobindo

There is yet another level of twinship extending far beyond the world of ordinary affairs yet with a surpassing world effect. That is the interaction between the Divine Father and the Divine Mother incarnated at the level of mastership. Supreme examples are Sri Aurobindo and the Mother (who died in 1950 and 1973, respectively). The work of these two rare beings, at their ashram and in their writings, conveys the sense of divinity that others perceived in them and that they worshiped in each other. Some Hindus believe that they were an incarnation of the Father and Mother aspects of God, Krishna, and Mahakali. In her childhood the Mother had visions of Aurobindo as Krishna. His teachings were centered upon her divinity as the Cosmic Mother, manifesting in different ways according to the plane upon which she is seen. At the same time, he wrote, "It is true of every soul on earth that it is a portion of the Divine Mother passing through the experiences of the Ignorance in order to arrive at the truth of its being and be the instrument of a Divine Manifestation and work here."

In truth, every pair of twin souls represents the Eternal Feminine and the Eternal Masculine, the Original Twins emergent from oneness. Through studying the lives of twin souls we arrive at a greater understanding of the God-force of love on which they are modeled. The identical pattern prevails in every pair, from the lowest status to the highest. We are given glimpses into the lives of Sri Aurobindo and the Mother in the book *Twelve Years with Sri Aurobindo,* by the Indian writer Nirodbaran. "'The Two who are one,'" Nirodbaran quotes Aurobindo as saying, "'are the secret of all power. The Two who are one are the might and right in things.'" He continues:

> There used to be considerable speculation in the early days about their mutual relationship. Was it one of Master and disciple or Shiva and Shakti? I was therefore very curious from the start to observe and discern the relationship. I came to the conclusion that it was that of Shiva and Shakti. The Mother has said, "Without him, I exist not; without me he is unmanifest." And we were given the unique opportunity of witnessing the dual personality of the One enacting on our earth plane an immortal drama, rare in the spiritual history of man. I could perfectly realize that without the Mother, Sri Aurobindo's stupendous realisations could not have taken such a concrete shape on this terrestrial base. In fact, he was waiting for the Mother's coming. He said that with the Mother's help he covered ten years of sadhana in one year.

They revered each other and deferred to each other in all things.

> If at any time we pressed our own opinion against the Mother's Sri Aurobindo would pull us up saying, "You think Mother does not know?" Similarly, if Sri Aurobindo passed some remark, the Mother would accept it as the last word. We used to hear her remark, "Sri Aurobindo said so." And Sri Aurobindo would quote the Mother's authority. To both of them, the other's word was law. One of us observed that only two persons have realized and put into practice Sri Aurobindo's Yoga of surrender: the Mother surrendering to Sri Aurobindo and Sri Aurobindo to the Mother.

They tended each other. The Mother was meticulous about every detail of his comfort, and he was equally solicitous about her well-being. He followed closely all her outer activities and enveloped her with an aura of protection against the dark forces. He asserted very firmly that their life was a battleground in a very real sense, and that he and the Mother were actively waging a continuous war against the adverse forces. The Mother said once that illnesses in their case were more than usually difficult to cure because of the concentrated attack of the adverse forces. Yet they guarded each other against any harm that could be caused by those forces. Says Nirodbaran, "Just as Sri Aurobindo used to protect the Mother, she protected him when needed: it was the role of the Lord and the Shakti. These are occult phenomena beyond our human intelligence."

They were the same, and yet complementary. The Mother's and Sri Aurobindo's talks were in vivid contrast.

> They sharply bring out the characteristics of two different personalities, though their consciousness is one. . . . Here the Mother's personality dominated the whole atmosphere; her tone, mood and manner were stamped with a seriousness, energy and force that demanded close attention. . . . The striking difference with Sri Aurobindo was his impersonality. . . . They were like a father and mother, both loving, but one indulgent, liberal, large, the other a firm though not inconsiderate disciplinarian. Both are aspects of the one Divine—Impersonal and Personal—and both have their ineffable charm.

The mutual surrender is characteristic of twinsoulship, as is the protectiveness on both sides, the reverence for the being of the other, and the strong, unique, complementary characters founded in oneness. High aspiration and service, so perfectly illustrated in these twin masters, will always be found in the completed pair. Taken together, they form the picture of spiritual love.

Sri Aurobindo teaches that all manifestation has been brought into being and is sustained by the Feminine of God. To uplift the heart and soul to the Divine Mother, the Universal Goddess, is to touch the true source of female power.

The Group Soul: Soul Mates

SOME OF OUR ACQUAINTANCES BECOME FRIENDS, some become good friends, a rare few become lifelong friends. With these few there is a sympathy and intuitive kinship that is beyond ordinary understanding.

There must be a reason for this. We believe it is that such people are true kin, members of our group soul, familiar to us from ages past. Our familiarity developed during the gestation period of creation, with the division of groups from the One. Though we speak of our group soul, ultimately there is no separate group to which we belong. We belong to all, for we were once a part of every group in the descent from the Source. Yet each group existed as a separate entity for an incalculable time on the descent into form. In its wholeness each group possessed a distinct character, and that character permeated the embryonic souls within it. The uniqueness of the group is forever reflected in those individuals whose formative prebirth occurred in its embrace.

Though all groups have cohered for infinite periods, some have cleaved together longer than others. The smaller the groups the longer the soul-cells within them have nestled together, absorbing each other's essence and growing alike, soul siblings in the womb of the Mother. These we will recognize as our soul mates.

The term "soul mates" is often used to mean twin souls, but there is an important distinction. Twins are two sides of the same soul, whereas group souls, though intimately related, are separate. We have many soul mates but only one twin soul; in the twins there is sameness, in the group similarity. But the similarities are profound.

Group-soul love springs from the same deep well as twin love; it comes to us already matured by virtue of the prolonged connection among the group members. When we encounter our group soul companions in this lifetime and quickly grow to love them, we find that the love has a different quality from the affections and passions we have known before. In group-soul love we find true compatibility and a harmony of like natures.

Our group may number in the hundreds, perhaps more, and is made up of diverse personalities. Yet we share an essential nature; for this reason others in our group soul are sometimes called *essence souls.* Our eyes are turned in the same direction, our steps follow the same path. Since we share a wholeness and a unique entity as a group, we are gifted in the same way. The gifts were assigned as we lay close to the heart of the cosmos. In our essence we are defined, for example, as the soul of music, or of art, science, invention, or healing.

Many of us have not yet discovered our gift. We may work at professions that are not allied to our talent, either through necessity or because the talents are not yet manifest. Nonetheless they are present, often sending us signals through our intuition, whispering to us in the still, small voice of the soul. They will reveal themselves as we grow in selfhood. Our soul mates will perhaps guide us to them, for we will share some aspects of the same gift, though with wide variations.

A clear line of demarcation separates one group soul from another, just as individuals are purposefully separate within the oneness of the whole. Only thus can they develop their uniqueness. Much later, like individual souls, the souls group will begin to flow into one another, when their identity is established and will not be lost in the All. The union that is the final goal is a union of fully realized Selves, added to but not absorbed in the ever-expanding Divine Self.

Here we see the reason for soul-grouping as part of the Divine Plan. We cannot find our way back to the Source by ourselves. We are not sufficient when made whole by our twin. We must ascend through a series of group completions, steps made of oneness upon oneness, and cemented with love. It is love that draws us back, love of humans while we are human: friendship love, family love, romantic love, passion love. Behind it all is soul love, the buried memory of the one soul that originally we were.

Our group soul mates may be friends, marriage partners, parents, children, lovers of the opposite or same sex. Homosexuality is a working out and evolvement of the gender proportions within the individual, no less than in heterosexual pairings. We view soul love between two men, two women, as group-soul love. These have chosen their path for valid reasons that as yet none can know, and they are helping to knit the group soul together, as are their other soul mates.

We are here to assist one another's evolution. That is the reason why many in a group, those who have need of one another at this time, have incarnated together. Given our individual freedoms, some in a group will be more advanced than others. These will aid the lesser evolved in their progress. The disparity in levels will not be great, however, for the group has been evolving as a loosely knit whole from its beginning. As it draws together and the souls become more nearly equal, it will ascend as a cohesive entity.

Here lies another distinction between group souls and twin souls. Group soul mates can be at somewhat different stages of evolution, unlike twin souls, who are certain to be equal in their evolved state. Because of their oneness of spirit, one twin will not be advanced beyond the other; though as free-willed individuals, one can urge the other onward or cause a delay for both.

Each group soul is made up of twins and twins-to-be. A prime aspect of the group work is bringing these pairs into alignment. It is matchmaking on a spiritual scale. And each reunited pair generates the pure energy that attracts more souls toward the group center. Thus there is no clear answer to the question "Do we meet the twin before the group?" The group unites the twins, and the twins further unite the group.

Here is one scenario. Twin souls met, and through studying their family in the light of group-soul knowledge, thought they perceived the soul mates that had been collecting round them. The woman felt that her parents belonged to her (and her twin's) group soul. She and her twin had both been married. She regarded one daughter among several as a soul mate; the man had a close soul connection with one of his sons and also with a nephew. When the woman was introduced to the son, they instinctively embraced, and the man felt the same kinship with her daughter. It seemed clear to them that the group soul round about them had predated their meeting and helped to prepare them for it.

The Law of Karma

Such a gathering of group souls in a family is dictated by individual and family karma. Karma means the return to us of everything that we have knowingly or unknowingly, wholly or in part, set into motion. The law is impersonal and entirely fair in its application.

Karma may be seen as the workings of a great body within the universal law. In Theosophical literature this is known as the *solar causal body.* We are all united on that level of higher intelligence; we are cells in that body, freely transmitting to one another. On the plane of the solar causal body, karma is ordained and orchestrated. Karmic intelligence arranges things for us, much the same way that the brain coordinates and arranges the functions for each of the organs of the body. Anything that we do to offend the solar causal body will call for adjustment and compensation, in the same way that homeostasis of the physical body reacts against any disturbance and works to restore equilibrium.

The response of our physical body to such a disruption is pain. The response of the solar causal body is also one of suffering, and that suffering is apportioned among us according to our deeds.

There is, however, a directing Mind of such benevolence that it turns back to us, many times multiplied, the effects of our good deeds while shaping every painful experience toward growth and increased happiness. We need fear no experience, only the refusal of experience.

Experience and the Group Soul

Sri Aurobindo asks why the growth of consciousness should be attended by so much ugliness and evil, spoiling the beauty of creation. In *Letters on Yoga* he answers:

> It need not have been so except for the overriding Will of the Supreme which meant that the possibilities of perversion by ignorance and the Dark Powers should be manifested in order to be eliminated through their being given their chance, since all possibility has to manifest somewhere. Once it is eliminated, the Divine Manifestation in matter will be greater than it otherwise could be, because it will combine all the possibilities involved in this difficult creation and not some of them as in an easier and less strenuous creation might naturally happen.

Yes, we live in a difficult creation, within worlds of infinite possibilities. We would wish it otherwise. But if we could see the whole picture in the heights of our souls' vision we would understand the purpose of anguish and pain and know that it is for ultimate good.

According to the ancient wisdom the soul must

acquire all experience on its way to perfection. *All* experience? Every soul? This is not possible, even in an eternity of time and infinity of space. God could have made it possible, of course, but evolved a better plan: the group soul.

Members of the group soul are one in essence. Experience, when distilled, enters into the essence of being and flows freely to the others. In a steady process of growth, the knowledge and the wisdom gained by the souls in their diversified living becomes part of the group as a whole. Such group sharing is a cosmic time-saver. By this plan all the burdens need not be assumed individually. In the end, each soul will be all-knowing, without having had to drink every cup to the bottom.

For as the group ascends to meet the next in the order of joining, it will become part of the greater oneness and subject to the same law of shared experience. And, the unions continuing across the broad spectrum of the universe, all experience will finally become common experience, while everything that makes each soul unique will persist.

There is a true story from the natural world that demonstrates the spirit of the group soul and the connection among its members.

The Hundreth Monkey

In the South Pacific there was a genius monkey. It is well known that monkeys love yams, but on that island the yams were too sandy to be eaten. This genius monkey took a yam and washed it in the edge of the sea, and then taught her family to do the same. Before long, other members of the tribe had been taught. When the hundredth monkey had learned the lesson, all the monkeys of that species on the island began to do the same. And soon the habit grew up among all those of the same species on the neighboring islands, which were inaccessible to one another. The experience of one had become the experience of the others.

The lesson is that there is a connection among members of a family, and through this communication the benefit of one is shared by all.

Group Karma

People often ask if the crippled, the blind, and the severely handicapped are paying the karmic price for crimes of the past. We believe that quite the reverse is probably true.

Karma works two ways: there is debit and credit. The hard roles in life are not given to the young souls but are chosen by the advanced ones. It is not for the karmic credit that these old souls take on the burden, but as an act of service, of gratitude for creation and for the gift of life.

Why else would children with Down's syndrome, people with cerebral palsy, or someone like Helen Keller radiate such great and shining spirits? By their example they are helping to lift the soul of humanity, a benefit that will endure while the pain of a handicapped existence is fleeting. Their sorrow is already alchemically transmuted to gold. And their group soul shares in the gold, the karmic credit which they bring to it as their offering of love.

A group soul will have karmic debts to pay as well. In uniting, they become responsible for one another. A serious misstep on the part of one in the group will require compensation by the whole.

Strong in union, no longer separate, they will pay these debts in a spirit of love and forgiveness, sharing the lessons and drawing closer as a result.

How many of our soul mates are we likely to meet in our lifetime? It is often said that we can count our true friends on the fingers of one hand. We are lucky, therefore, if we have found a handful of soul mates. Yet many may be gathering around us, and we must be ready to recognize and receive them. Recognizing the soul mate is similar to recognizing the twin. A destiny is fulfilled as we make conscious connection with one from whom we have long been parted. It follows that we are then lifted to new heights of happiness.

Twin- and group-soul reunions can be expected to keep pace with each other. The increasing number of twin-soul meetings that are beginning to occur will be paralleled by more frequent recognitions within the group.

Recognizing the Soul Mate

The recognition of the soul mate begins inwardly. Soul connections are made on the inner planes of being. As we open ourselves to that possibility we help to create its outer manifestation. Only after we have become attuned to our soul mates on subtle levels will they appear before us. Then we will recognize the soul in the person, or more properly the person within the soul.

When we meet a soul mate there will be an immediate liking between us. As we grow in friendship we will discover that we see eye to eye on most subjects of importance. Our interests may be quite different, but our attitude toward life will be the same. We will have a similar moral sense, with a forgiveness for others' faults and an awareness of our own, a sense of mission in life, and the recognition of purpose in all life. These are qualities of soul, and when our communion occurs at soul level, there will be an unbroken flow of harmony, despite differences in personality. The very breadth of those differences will excite our interest in one another and allow for the expansiveness of the group.

We will not feel jealous of one another, as in lesser friendships. We will be happy in one another's presence. There will be love and energy exchange between us, akin to the energy generated between twin souls. In many ways the pattern is repeated with twin and group souls, except that twin souls are always of the opposite sex, whereas soul mates are of both.

And again, our preparation for our soul mates is the same as for our twin: the development of self. Yet self-development is the beginning, not the end. There are those who insist that the way to salvation lies wholly within the self. But finally we all must ask, "What is my selfhood for?" The soul will answer, "It is for the other."

The purpose of our self-development is that we may learn to love. Were it not for the love of others, we would be closed in with ourselves forever. Some would say, "As I find myself, I can love others." Yes, but love as we know it is partial. It travels on a two-way track, from me to you and from you to me. We remain separated. There is a space between us. That is where our shadow side stands ready to invade. It is there that so many lovers are cut down and that their love is deflected onto the long slide toward hate.

The wholeness of love occurs only when I become you and you become me. That is supreme empathic bonding. That is soul-love and the way of complete understanding. It comes in the union with our twin and our group. Our growth in love is all for this. Our pursuit of self-improvement is a growth of love.

That growth is seen across society these days as the age of Aquarius gains momentum. People are drawing together in countless ways for self-improvement and discovery. One method is group therapy. Though approached from self-need, boundaries among members are dissolved, showing us that people can come together in an arbitrarily formed group and behave very much like group souls.

Coauthor Maurie Pressman illustrates this point with the following history from his psychiatrist's casebook:

> Gail had been raised by elderly parents who were
> extremely distant, emotionally. When she joined
> a therapy group she was forty-five and single,
> though she had been looking all her life for a deep
> and fulfilling relationship. Indeed it was her failure
> to connect that had brought her to my door. During one session she told the group she wanted to

leave for another, where she might be better understood and have a deeper experience.

I realized that what she was really saying was, "I want to get into my deeper feelings so that I can be fully understood." I said to her, "I think you are bringing out the deeper feeling you want to get into. It's the feeling that you'll never be understood—even your parents never understood you. I think this is the theme of your life." She replied: "But you can never be completely understood." Something made me say, "Yes you can." I was thinking, of course, in spiritual terms.

Gail said, "If I can't be completely understood I'd rather not try at all, I'd rather stay away." I considered, then told her, "I can understand that— but by keeping yourself at a distance you make complete understanding impossible. That's why you're so lonely. You've had one of the most lonely lives I have ever heard of." I could see the sadness in Gail's eyes and I said, "There it is. You're feeling sad now, are you not?" She admitted that she was. I said, "Let it come, let it come." Tears began to roll down her cheeks. Another woman patient reached out and took her hand, and I moved over and held her other hand, quietly whispering, "Keep it coming, keep it coming." And so she cried, this woman who normally was jacketed in defensive armor. The tears continued to flow for some time. Finally she took a deep breath and said she felt a healing.

I said to her, "This is part of being completely understood. And how much better you look! How beautiful you look!" For she did; she was transformed. I looked around and saw that everybody's face was aglow—with happiness, a kind of joyous sympathy, and love. I told her to look at these faces. "See what you've done for them as well as yourself." I then spoke about this love in the room as being spiritual and true. "*This* is spirituality. This is what the world can be like. This joy and this love are what come forth after the false skin of conditioning is melted."

Such groups provide useful "practice" for true group souls on the pathway.

The Family Group

The best-known form of practice for union is obtained in the family.

The earthly family is a preparatory ground, albeit at times a battleground, for the soul's learning. An inbuilt difficulty for families is that the individuals within them so often seem to be at varying levels of evolution. We believe that this is an ordained imbalance of soul strengths, and that in meeting the challenge, the more developed family members are intended to lift the lesser.

Do the genetic family and the soul family coincide? Not generally. With advanced evolution, however, the soul can choose its human family before incarnating; thus it can happen that two or more from a group soul are born into the same earthly family. Such a gift comes with its own share of difficulties. Perhaps one parent and one child are from the same group soul, which results in the two having a special bond; this may generate feelings of jealousy and reactive guilt among the others. There is almost always some favoritism in a family, with the attendant pain and guilt. How much easier it would be if people could know that the basic reason for their fondnesses is the positions of their souls in the tapestry of the heavens!

While group souls may incarnate within a family, twin souls never do. There would be incestuous implications if such were to happen. On this account we feel certain that twins will never incarnate as parent and child or brother and sister. The union of twin souls is a love union in the fullest sense; with reason, they have been termed in one biography "the Immortal Lovers." They are mates, finely fashioned vehicles for experiencing sexual polarity and gender attraction.

Although some families may contain like souls, there are others that seem to consist of souls from different universes. Here there is intolerable conflict and tension, the antithesis of the empathic understanding that comes naturally to those in a near group. The powers of darkness capitalize on the strife, fostering lives of misery, drug and alcohol addiction, child abuse, wife battering, suicide, and murder.

It may be that their evolution is being forced. Perhaps they have been resistant to growth. By cosmic law we evolve willingly or by force, a choice that the universe allows. If we are unwilling, our evolution is forced upon us and brings the sorrow and tragedy that will wake us up. At the same time we can know that every individual is of the same divine lineage as everyone else and is regarded as sacred by the Lords of karma, who bring all arrangements into being and into perfect balance on the scales of justice.

Married couples who appear to be worlds apart in fact may be. They will be from soul groups far apart in the schematic design but will have been brought together as purposefully as the twin souls or group lovers, even if not paired for the joy of union. Aside from their karmic learning, such seemingly ill-suited couples might be serving to bridge their distant groups. Someday they may meet again as soul mates, having helped lead others toward that union.

The impulse of all that has been created is toward union, whatever the pace. All groups, clubs, organizations, and collectives are following an inner drive to cohere and return. Their activities accord with the strengthening will to goodness throughout evolving life. Groups with an altruistic purpose are a feature of the later centuries, ours especially: the Salvation Army, the Theosophical Society, the Humane Society, Red Cross, Alcoholics Anonymous, and countless others. We also see the rapid spread of the human rights movement.

Those organizations have their evil counterparts. Neo-Nazis, white supremacists, and international terrorist organizations also obey the call to union. But the mission of their union is to further the cause of separation. Yet the forces of separatism will not endure. Darkness has its day and passes; it is not of the evolving stream.

Advanced Group Souls in Service

The ascension and assembly of group souls steadily illumine the human scene. Evidence of this is the tremendous group displays of service to humanity through the centuries. Advanced souls have periodically descended in group incarnation, elevating the race by quantum leaps in art or science, or satisfying the thirsting soul of humanity with music, the direct voice of God.

Group identity revealed itself with the touching down of the great composers, giants such as Bach, Haydn, Beethoven, Mozart, and Brahms. They and others of their soul group rendered a gift of musical creation the like of which the world has never known.

Then too there was the collective soul of the master painters: da Vinci, Michelangelo, Raphael, and others, who all came into incarnation within a brief time of one another. In the gift of their creations, these greats illustrated the return of like to like in the highly evolved group soul.

So, also, did the great thinkers, another highly evolved group soul, which elected to incarnate and open the world of science to a groping humanity. It required time for the revelations of Copernicus and Galileo to be absorbed, but the pace accelerated with the arrival of Darwin, Newton, and Einstein. Newton, perhaps the greatest of them all, hardly entered into human life at all but merely stood apart, contributing. He mirrors his lost heaven with these words, written shortly before his death: "I do not know what I may appear to the world, but to myself I seem to have been only like a boy playing on the seashore and diverting myself in now and then finding a smoother pebble or a prettier shell than ordinary, whilst the great ocean of truth lay all undiscovered before me."

The group soul of psychology brought to our midst another wave of like souls, spearheaded by Freud and followed by such greats as Jung, Adler, Rank, and Reich. Because they are closer to us in time, we are made aware of dissonances and jealousies among these kindred souls. For instance, Jung was Freud's announced heir apparent, his undisputed favorite. But when Jung eventually diverged from his mentor, a major schism developed between the two. Jung followed his own path, which Freud called "too religious." Jung, in turn, judged Freud to be autocratic and to have a closed mind. The truths of their separate visions were from a high plane, the causes for the parting from a lesser-evolved personality level.

Such examples of human frailty in the lives of the towering composers, painters, and scientists show us that our foibles will not pass away automatically as we join our group. Union is a process, not an instant occurrence. The same is true of twin-soul unions. There is much creative work to do in the melding of strong souls, who must learn to maintain individuality while moving toward oneness.

Gender and Consciousness

From a group soul of poetry we single out two poets, Walt Whitman and Edward Carpenter, for what they can teach us of gender in relation to the group soul. There were great similarities in their lives. Both had taken the homosexual path in this life and both were cosmic consciousness illuminates. Each produced one masterwork, an entire book of poetry expressing the bliss consciousness: Whitman's *Leaves of Grass*, Carpenter's *Towards Democracy*. Plainly their mission was to make cosmic consciousness known as the universal condition. They incarnated contemporaneously: Carpenter in England and Whitman in America; later they met briefly as famous men.

Both poets showed a high advancement of their inner masculine and feminine, the forceful creative power of the yang, well balanced with yin sensitivities. They were not impelled to seek the twin soul in their lifetime. We believe that at such an evolutionary level the twin will already have been found and will be overseeing the life, inspiring the work, and expanding the consciousness from higher planes.

The sexual impulse of the grounded twin will be put to use in the soul development of the group. The group necessity is to develop all aspects of itself in its evolution as a complete entity. Every soul within it is concerned with realizing and proportioning its gender powers, and the group soul collectively must do the same. Its yin and yang energies evolve themselves through benign activity in human beings of both sexes.

The soul-substance shared by group members is comparable to the genes in a family. As the group souls fuse in harmony, the soul-substance flows more freely among them; boundaries lessen, they become more and more each other, more and more themselves, and more expanded in love. Group love still retains the individual signatures that have contributed to its evolution. Each separate wedding of souls has infused more power into the whole.

Love among group soul mates can be extremely powerful, duplicating in many ways the love between twins. The strength of love-energy among group members is, we believe, paralleled by their placement in the group.

The universe, we know, is built upon mathematical principles. "God ever geometrizes," wrote da Vinci. When we consider the analogy between the separation of cells in the fertilized ovum and the creative divisions of souls, we can envision the mathematical sequence of the group separations, each group divided repeatedly into halves. As they were divided, so they will return. The gathering together of group souls on the stairway of return cannot be random, any more than separated twin souls could randomly unite with any other. The orderly reassembling of souls reflects the orderly plan of the universe. We will return in reverse order of our descent.

As there was an order to the separation of groups, so there is an order of souls within the group itself. We can find corroboration of this in our own lives. Among a number of friends who could be soul mates, we will be aware of a closer bond with some than with others. That has to do with our positioning in the group. Those who were later in separating are closer in love. The two pairs of twins that were the last to separate from each other are very closely related: they are next-of-twin. When they meet in human incarnation, their love is second only to the love of twins.

The great love stories in literature and life have always centered upon twin souls. But there is a new kind of love story forming, one that expands the old framework. It is the group-soul love story. This is the true life story of our advancing souls, depicting a love grander and more powerful than any we have known or could have conceived. It is love multiplied by the number of soul-participants, flowing back into each with the accumulated force of joy.

Literature often provides the clearest confirmation of great truths. All that is said here about group souls is summed up by Katherine Anne Porter in an episode from her novel *Pale Horse, Pale Rider.* A young woman desperately ill with influenza at the time of World War I goes briefly over the edge into death and meets her group souls.

> The small waves rolled in and over unhurriedly, lapped upon the sand in silence and retreated; the grasses flurried before a breeze that made no sound. Moving towards her leisurely as clouds through the shimmering air came a

great company of human beings, and Miranda saw in an amazement of joy that they were all the living she had known. Their faces were transfigured, each in its own beauty, beyond what she remembered of them, their eyes were clear and untroubled as good weather, and they cast no shadows. They were pure identities and she knew them every one without calling their names or remembering what relation she bore to them. They surrounded her smoothly on silent feet, then turned their entranced faces again towards the sea, and she moved among them easily as a wave among waves. The drifting circle widened, separated, and each figure was alone but not solitary; Miranda, alone too, questioning nothing, desiring nothing, in the quietude of her ecstasy, stayed where she was, eyes fixed on the overwhelming deep sky where it was always morning.

Afterword

ALL THAT HAS BEEN SAID HERE ABOUT TWIN souls relates to you. Whatever your circumstance, whether of loneliness, despair, pain through love's betrayal, you can know that you are indissolubly linked with another who shares your burden. Together, though seemingly apart, you and your twin struggle with purpose through the darkness of this world, surrounded by the unseen spiritual light. Your meeting is destined. You cannot know the place or the time, but suddenly you will round a corner, the clouds will lift, the light will break over you and you will be in each other's sight.

There is nothing more certain than that.

Permissions

The authors gratefully acknowledge permission to reprint passages from the following:

The Letters of Abélard and Héloïse, translated by Betty Radice. Copyright ©1974 by Penguin, U.K. Reprinted by permission of the publisher.

Love and Sexuality: Complete Works, Part I by Omraam Mikhaël Aïvanhov. Copyright ©1988 by Omraam Mikhaël Aïvanhov. Reprinted by permission of Prosveta, Los Angeles.

The Synthesis of Yoga by Sri Aurobindo. Copyright ©1976 by Sri Aurobindo. Reprinted by permission of Sri Aurobindo Ashram, Pondicherry, India.

The Secret Doctrine by Helena Blavatsky. Copyright ©1888 by Helena Blavatsky. Reprinted by permission of Theosophical Publishing House, Wheaton, Ill.

Index

About the Authors

PATRICIA JOUDRY is a playwright, novelist, educator, and sound therapist. Her plays have been performed on Broadway and throughout Canada, the United States, and Europe. Her novel *The Selena Tree* is to appear as a television miniseries in her native Canada.

She is the innovator of a self-help listening technique founded on the work of Dr. Alfred A. Tomatis, which aids learning, rehabilitates the ear, and recharges the brain. Her book *Sound Therapy for the Walkman* has provided help for people with hearing disabilities in forty-nine countries.

In addition, she pioneered the home-school movement, educating her children at home in the Cotswold Hills of England in the 1960s. Her recently completed autobiography, *My Life as Patricia Joudry* tells of her battles with school authorities and attacks sustained by powers of darkness. She has been receiving spiritual guidance on the little-known principle of twin souls since the 1960s, and this has become the central work of her life.

Joudry has five daughters, two of whom are continuing her work with sound therapy in Canada and Australia. She lives alone, close to nature, in a cabin on the sea in British Columbia, Canada.

MAURIE D. PRESSMAN, M.D., is the medical director and founder of the Pressman Center for Mind/Body Wellness, a clinic that focuses on spiritual psychotherapy and the exploration of the human soul. Dr. Pressman has studied the potential of the human mind and soul for more than forty years, creating a bridge between traditional psychiatry and wholistic spiritual psychotherapy. He has taught sports science at the University of Delaware and has pioneered the use of hypnosis and creative visualization work with Olympic ice skaters. He has also done extensive research on death and dying, behavior genetics, and learning disabilities.

He is clinical professor of psychiatry at Temple University and emeritus chairman of psychiatry at the Albert Einstein Medical Center. For the past two and a half years, he has been a monthly columnist in the *Monthly Aspectarian,* a prestigious new age journal published in Chicago. His most recent book, *Enter the Supermind,* gives case illustrations of how people have experienced the Supermind through personal development.

Hazelden Transitions is an initiative between Hazelden Foundation's Information and Educational Services division and Transitions Bookplace, Inc.

Hazelden Information and Educational Services helps individuals, families, and communities prevent and/or recover from alcoholism, drug addiction, and other related diseases and conditions. We do this by partnering with authors and other experts to deliver information and educational products and services that customers use to aid their personal growth and change, leading along a wholistic pathway of hope, health, and abundant living. We are fortunate to be recognized by both professionals and consumers as the leading international center of resources in these areas.

Transitions Bookplace, Inc., founded in Chicago, Illinois, in 1989, has become the nation's leading independent bookseller dedicated to customers seeking personal growth and development. Customers can choose from more than thirty thousand books, videos, pamphlets, and musical selections. Authors appear frequently for special events or workshops in the Transitions Learning Center. Also available in the store is a legendary collection of exquisite international gifts celebrating body, mind, and spirit.

This Hazelden Transitions Bookplace initiative is dedicated to all brave souls who seek to change courses in their lives, their families, and their communities in order to achieve hope, health, and abundant living.

Transitions Bookplace
1000 West North Avenue
Chicago, IL 60622
312-951-READ
800-979-READ
www.transitionsbookplace.com

Hazelden Information and Educational Services
15251 Pleasant Valley Road
Center City, MN 55012-0176
800-328-9000
www.hazelden.org